D0655431

What I Know
For Sure

What I Know
For Sure

Oprah Winfrey

MACMILLAN

First published 2014 in the US as *What I Know For Sure* by Flatiron Books

First published in the UK 2014 by Macmillan
an imprint of Pan Macmillan
20 New Wharf Road, London N1 9RR
Associated companies throughout the world
www.panmacmillan.com

ISBN 978-1-4472-7766-8

What I Know For Sure Copyright © 2014 by Hearst Communications, Inc. All rights reserved.

Book designed by Kathryn Parise

The right of Oprah Winfrey to be identified as the
author of this work has been asserted by her in accordance
with the Copyright, Designs and Patents Act 1988.

All the essays included in this book were previously published,
in a slightly different form, in *O, The Oprah Magazine*.

O, The Oprah Magazine and 'What I Know For Sure'
are registered trademarks of Harpo Print, LLC.

Lyrics from 'Stand' reprinted with the permission of Donnie McClurkin.
Letter from Mattie J. T. Stepanek reprinted by permission of Mattie J. T. Stepanek,
personal communication (www.MattieOnline.com). Edna St. Vincent Millay, excerpt
from 'On Thought in Harness' from *Collected Poems*. Copyright © 1934, 1962 by Edna St.
Vincent Millay and Norma Millay Ellis. Reprinted with the permission of The Permissions
Company, Inc., on behalf of Holly Peppe, Literary Executor, The Millay Society, www.millay.org.
'You Ask About Poetry' reprinted with the permission of Mark Nepo. Excerpt from 'Love After
Love' from *The Poetry of Derek Walcott 1948–2013* by Derek Walcott, selected by Glyn Maxwell.
Copyright © 2014 by Derek Walcott. Reprinted by permission of Farrar, Straus and Giroux, LLC.

All rights reserved. No part of this publication may be reproduced,
stored in or introduced into a retrieval system, or transmitted, in any form,
or by any means (electronic, mechanical, photocopying, recording or otherwise)
without the prior written permission of the publisher. Any person who does
any unauthorized act in relation to this publication may be liable to
criminal prosecution and civil claims for damages.

Pan Macmillan has no responsibility for the information provided by any
author websites whose address you obtain from this book ('author websites').
The inclusion of author website addresses in this book does not constitute
an endorsement by or association with us of such sites or the content,
products, advertising or other materials presented on such sites.

10

A CIP catalogue record for this book is available from the British Library.

Printed and bound by CPI Group (UK) Ltd, Croydon, CR0 4YY

Visit **www.panmacmillan.com** to read more about all our books
and to buy them. You will also find features, author interviews and
news of any author events, and you can sign up for e-newsletters
so that you're always first to hear about our new releases.

South Dublin Libraries

www.southdublinlibraries.ie

Introduction

It's not a new story, but at least for this book, I think it's worth telling one last time: The year was 1998, I had been promoting the movie *Beloved* in a live television interview with the late, great *Chicago Sun-Times* film critic, Gene Siskel, and everything was going perfectly smoothly, until the time came to wrap things up. "Tell me," he asked, "what do you know for sure?"

Now, this was not my first rodeo. I've asked and been asked an awful lot of questions over the years, and it isn't often that I find myself at a complete loss for words—but I have to say, the man managed to stop me in my tracks.

"Uhhhhh, about the movie?" I stammered, knowing full well that he was after something bigger, deeper, more complex, but trying to stall until I could come up with a semi-coherent response.

"No," he said. "You know what I mean—about you, your life, anything, everything . . . "

"Uhhhh, I know for sure . . . uhhh . . . I know for sure, I need time to think about that some more, Gene."

Well, sixteen years and a great deal of thought later, it has become the central question of my life: At the end of the day, what exactly do I know for sure?

I've explored that question in every issue of O magazine—in fact, "What I Know for Sure" is the name of my monthly column—and believe me, there are still plenty of times when an answer doesn't come easy. What do I know for sure? I know that if one more editor calls or e-mails or even sends a smoke signal asking where this month's installment is, I'm going to change my name and move to Timbuktu!

But just when I'm ready to raise the white flag and yell, "That's it! I'm tapped out! I know nothing!" I'll find myself walking the dogs or brewing a pot of chai or soaking in the tub, when, out of nowhere, a little moment of crystal clarity will bring me back to something that in my head and my heart and my gut, I absolutely do know beyond a shadow of a doubt.

Still, I have to admit that I was a bit apprehensive when it came to rereading fourteen years' worth of columns. Would it be like looking back at old photos of me in haircuts and outfits that really ought to be left in the seemed-like-a-good-idea-at-the-time file? I mean, what do you do if what you knew for sure back in the day turns into *what were you thinking*, here in the present?

I took a red pen, a glass of Sauvignon Blanc, a deep breath, sat down, and started to read. And as I read, what I was doing and where I was in my life when I wrote these pieces came flooding back. I instantly remembered wracking my brain and searching my soul, sitting up late and waking up early, all to figure out what I've come to understand about the things that matter in life, things like joy, resilience, awe, connection, gratitude, and possibility. I'm happy to report that what I discovered in those fourteen years of columns is that when you know something, *really* know something, it tends to stand the test of time.

Don't get me wrong: You live, and if you're open to the world, you learn. So while my core thinking remains pretty solid, I did wind up using that red pen to nip and tuck, explore and expand a few old truths and some hard-earned insights. Welcome to my own private book of revelations!

As you read about all the lessons I've struggled with, cried over, run from, circled back to, made peace with, laughed about, and at long last come to know for sure, my hope is that you'll begin to ask yourself the very same question Gene Siskel asked me all those years ago. I know that what you'll find along the way will be fantastic, because what you'll find will be yourself.

Joy

———— ❦ ————

"Sit. Feast on your life."

—Derek Walcott

The first time Tina Turner appeared on my show, I wanted to run away with her, be a backup girl, and dance all night at her concerts. Well, that dream came true one night in L.A. when *The Oprah Winfrey Show* went on tour with Tina. After a full day's rehearsal for just one song, I got my chance.

It was the most nerve-racking, knee-shaking, exhilarating experience ever. For 5 minutes and 27 seconds I got a chance to feel what it's like to rock onstage. I have never been more out of my element, out of my body. I remember counting the steps in my head, trying to keep the rhythm, waiting for the big kick, and being so self-conscious.

Then, in an instant, it dawned on me: *Okay, girl, this is going to be over soon.* And if I didn't loosen up, I would miss the fun. So I threw my head back, forgot about step, step, turn, kick, and just danced. *WHEEEEW!*

Several months later I received a package from my friend and mentor Maya Angelou—she'd said she was sending me a gift she'd want any daughter of hers to have. When I ripped it open, I found a CD of a song by Lee Ann Womack that I can still hardly listen to without boohooing. The song, which is a testament to Maya's life, has this line as its refrain: *When you get the choice to sit it out or dance, I hope you dance.*

What I know for sure is that every day brings a chance for you to draw in a breath, kick off your shoes, and step out and dance—to live free of regret and filled with as much joy, fun, and laughter as you can stand. You can either waltz boldly onto the stage of life and live the way you know your spirit is nudging you to, or you can sit quietly by the wall, receding into the shadows of fear and self-doubt.

You have the choice this very moment—the only moment you have for certain. I hope you aren't so wrapped up in nonessential stuff that you forget to really enjoy yourself—because this moment is about to be over. I hope you'll look back and remember today as the day you decided to make every one count, to relish each hour as if there would never be another. And when you get the choice to sit it out or dance, I hope you dance.

I *take my pleasures* seriously. I work hard and play well; I believe in the yin and yang of life. It doesn't take a lot to make me happy because I find satisfaction in so much of what I do. Some satisfactions are higher-rated than others, of course. And because I try to practice what I preach—living in the moment—I am consciously attuned most of the time to how much pleasure I am receiving.

How many times have I laughed so hard on the phone with my best friend, Gayle King, that my head started to hurt? Mid-howl I sometimes think, *Isn't this a gift—after so many years of nightly phone calls, to have someone who tells me the truth and to laugh this loudly about it?* I call that five-star pleasure.

Being aware of, and creating, four- and five-star experiences makes you blessed. For me, just waking up "clothed in my right mind," being able to put my feet on the floor, walk to the bathroom, and do what needs to be done there is five stars. I've heard many stories of people who aren't healthy enough to do that.

A strong cup of coffee with the perfect hazelnut creamer: four stars. Going for a walk through the woods with the dogs unleashed: five stars. Working out: one star, still. Sitting under my oaks, reading the Sunday papers: four stars. A great book: five. Hanging out at Quincy Jones's kitchen table, talking about everything and nuthin': five stars. Being able to do good things for other people: five plus. The enjoyment comes from knowing the receiver understands the spirit of the gift. I make an effort to do something good for somebody every day, whether I know that person or not.

What I know for sure is that pleasure is energy reciprocated: What you put out comes back. Your base level of pleasure is determined by how you view your whole life.

More important than 20/20 eyesight is your internal vision, your own sweet spirit whispering through your life with guidance and grace—now that's pleasure.

L*ife is full of* delightful treasures, if we take a moment to appreciate them. I call them *ahhh* moments, and I've learned how to create them for myself. Case in point: my 4 p.m. cup of masala chai tea (spicy, hot, with foamed almond milk on top—it's refreshing and gives me a little lift for the rest of the afternoon). Moments like this are powerful, I know for sure. They can be your recharge, your breathing space, your chance to reconnect with *you*.

I have *always adored* the word *delicious*. The way it rolls off my tongue delights me. And even more delectable than a delicious meal is a delicious experience, rich and layered like a fine coconut cake. I had one a few birthdays ago—both the cake and the experience. It was one of those moments I call a God wink—when out of the blue everything lines up just perfectly.

I was hanging out with a group of girlfriends in Maui; I'd just come back from India and wanted to have a spa retreat at my house to celebrate turning 58.

As girlfriends do even at this age, we sat around the table and talked till midnight. On the night before my birthday, five of the eight of us were still at the table at 12:30 a.m., worn out from a five-hour conversation that had run the gamut from men to microdermabrasion. Lots of laughing, some tears. The kind of talking women do when we feel safe.

In two days I was scheduled to interview the famed

spiritual teacher Ram Dass, and by coincidence I started to hum a line from a song invoking his name.

Suddenly my friend Maria said, "What's that you're humming?"

"Oh, just a line from a song I like."

She said, "I know that song. I listen to it *every* night."

"No way," I said. "It's an obscure song on an album by a woman named Snatum Kaur."

"Yes!" Maria said. "Yes! Yes! Snatum Kaur! I listen to her every night before I go to bed. How do you know her music?"

"Peggy"—another friend who was with us—"gave me a CD two years ago, and I've been listening ever since. I play her every day before meditating."

Now we were both screaming and laughing. "No *way!*"

"I actually thought of having her come to sing for my birthday," I said when I caught my breath. "Then I went, *Nah, too much trouble.* Had I known you liked her, too, I would have made the effort."

Later that night, lying in bed, I thought, *Isn't that something. I would have gone to the trouble for a friend but not for myself. For sure I need to practice what I preach and value myself more*. I went to sleep wishing I'd invited Snatum Kaur to sing.

The next day, my birthday, we had a "land blessing" with a Hawaiian chieftain. That evening we gathered on the porch for sunset cocktails. My friend Elizabeth stood up—to read a poem, I thought, or make a speech. Instead she said, "You wanted it, and now you have manifested it." She rang a small chime, and suddenly music started to play.

The music was muffled, as if the speakers weren't working. I thought, *What's going on?* And then there appeared, walking onto my front porch . . . Snatum Kaur, in her white turban. And her musicians! "How did this happen?" I cried. And cried, and *cried*. Maria, sitting next to me with tears in her eyes, held my hand and just nodded. "You wouldn't do it for yourself, so we did it for you."

After I'd gone to bed the night before, my friends had called to find out where Snatum Kaur was, to see if they could get her to Maui in the next 12 hours. As life and God would have it, she and her musicians were in a town 30 minutes away, preparing for a concert. And were "honored" to come and sing.

It was one of the most amazing surprises of my life. Layered with meanings I'm still deciphering. What I know for sure: It's a moment I'll savor forever—the fact that it happened, the way it happened, that it happened on my birthday. All . . . so . . . *delicious*!

When *was the last time* you laughed with a friend till your sides hurt or dropped the kids off with a sitter and went away for an entire weekend? More to the point, if your life ended tomorrow, what would you regret not doing? If this were the last day of your life, would you spend it the way you're spending today?

I once passed a billboard that caught my attention. It read, "He who dies with the most toys is still dead." Anyone who has ever come close to death can tell you that at the end of your life, you probably won't be reminiscing about how many all-nighters you pulled at the office or how much your mutual fund is worth. The thoughts that linger are the "if only" questions, like *Who could I have become if I had finally done the things I always wanted to do?*

The gift of deciding to face your mortality without turning away or flinching is the gift of recognizing that because you will die, you must live now. Whether you flounder or flourish is always in your hands—you are the single biggest influence in your life.

Your journey begins with a choice to get up, step out, and live fully.

Is *there anything I love* more than a good meal? Not much. One of my best took place on a trip to Rome, at a delightful little restaurant filled exclusively with Italians except for our table: my friends Reggie, Andre, and Gayle, Gayle's daughter Kirby, and me, eating as the Romans do.

There was a moment when the waiters, prompted by our Italian host, Angelo, brought out so many delicious antipasti that I actually felt my heart surge, like an engine switching gears. We had zucchini stuffed with prosciutto, and fresh, ripe tomatoes layered with melting mozzarella so warm you could see tiny cheese bubbles, along with a bottle of '85 Sassicaia, a Tuscan red wine that had been breathing for half an hour, to sip and savor like liquid velvet. Oh my, these were moments to treasure!

Did I mention I topped all this off with a bowl of pasta e fagioli (made to perfection) and a little tiramisu? Yep, that was some good eating. I paid for it with a 90-minute jog around the Colosseum the next day—but it was worth every delectable bite.

I have a lot of strong beliefs. The value of eating well is one of them. I know for sure that a meal that brings you real joy will do you more good in the long and short term than a lot of filler food that leaves you standing in your kitchen, roaming from cabinet to fridge. I call it the grazing feeling: You want something, but can't figure out what it is. All the carrots, celery, and skinless chicken in the world can't give you the satisfaction of one incredible piece of chocolate if that's what you really crave.

So I've learned to eat one piece of chocolate—maximum, two—and dare myself to stop and relish it, knowing full well, like Scarlett O'Hara, that "tomorrow is another day," and there's always more where that came from. I don't have to consume the whole thing just because it's there. What a concept!

I*t's been more than* two decades since I first met Bob Greene at a gym in Telluride, Colorado. I weighed 237 pounds at the time, my highest ever. I was at the end of my rope and the end of hope—so ashamed of my body and my eating habits, I could barely look Bob in the eye. I desperately wanted a solution that worked.

Bob put me through my workout paces and encouraged a lifestyle built around eating whole foods (long before I'd ever heard of the store that shares that name and mission).

I resisted. But even as different diets came and went, his advice remained consistent and wise: Eat foods that make you thrive.

A few years ago, I finally got the big aha and started growing my own vegetables. And what began with a few rows of lettuce, some tomatoes, and basil (my favorite herb) in my backyard in Santa Barbara eventually became a genuine farm in Maui. My gardening interest grew into a passion.

I get ridiculously happy at the sight of the purple radicchio we've grown, the elephant kale that reaches my knees, the radishes so big I call them baboon butts—because for me it all represents a full-circle moment.

In rural Mississippi, where I was born, a garden meant survival. In Nashville, where I later lived, my father always cleared a "patch" by the side of our house, where he would grow collard greens, tomatoes, crowder peas, and butter beans.

Today that's my favorite meal; add some cornbread and I'm clicking my heels. But when I was a girl, I saw no value in eating freshly grown foods. "Why can't we have store-bought food like other people?" I'd complain. I wanted my vegetables to come from the "valley of the jolly—ho, ho, ho—Green Giant"! Having to eat from the garden made me feel poor.

I now know for sure how blessed I was to have access to fresh food—something not every family today can take for granted.

Thank you, Lord, for growth.

I've worked hard to sow the seeds for a life in which I get to keep expanding my dreams. One of those dreams is for everyone to be able to eat fresh food that goes from farm to table—because better food is the foundation for a better life. Yes, Bob, I'm putting it in print: You were right all along!

I met *Gayle King* in 1976, when I was a news anchor at a station in Baltimore and she was a production assistant—both of us from circles that rarely interacted and certainly weren't friendly. From the day we met, Gayle made it known how proud she was that I had the exalted position of anchorwoman and how excited she was to be part of a team I was on. It has been that way ever since.

We didn't become friends right away—we were just two women respectful and supportive of each other's path. Then one night, after a big snowstorm, Gayle couldn't get home—so I invited her to stay at my place. Her biggest concern? Underwear. She was determined to drive 40 miles through a snowstorm to get to Chevy Chase, Maryland, where she lived with her mom, in order to have clean panties. "I have lots of clean underwear," I told her. "You can use mine, or we can go buy you some."

Once I finally convinced her to come home with me, we stayed up the whole night talking. And with the exception of a few times during vacations spent out of the country, Gayle and I have talked every day since.

We laugh a lot, mostly about ourselves. She has helped me through demotions, near-firings, sexual harassment, and the twisted and messed-up relationships of my twenties, when I couldn't tell the difference between myself and a doormat. Night after night, Gayle listened to the latest woeful tale of how I'd been stood up, lied to, done wrong. She'd always ask for details (we call it "book, chapter, and verse"), then seem as engaged as if it were happening to her. She never judged me. Yet when I'd let some man use me, she'd often say, "He's just chipping away at your spirit. One day I hope he chips deep enough for you to see who you really are—someone who deserves to be happy."

In all my triumphs—in every good and great thing that has ever happened to me—Gayle has been my boldest cheerleader. (Of course, no matter how much money I make, she still worries that I'm spending too much. "Remember M.C. Hammer," she chides, as though I'm one purchase away from following in the footsteps of the rapper who went bankrupt.) And in all our years together,

I have never sensed even a split second of jealousy from her. She loves her life, she loves her family, she loves discount shopping (enough to schlep across town for a sale on Tide).

Only once has she admitted to wanting to trade places with me: the night I sang onstage with Tina Turner. She, who cannot carry a tune in a church pew, fantasizes about being a singer.

Gayle is the nicest person I know—genuinely interested in everybody's story. She's the kind of person who will ask a cabdriver in New York City if he has any kids. "What are their names?" she'll say. When I'm down, she shares my pain; when I'm up, you can believe she's somewhere in the background, cheering louder and smiling broader than anyone else. Sometimes I feel like Gayle is the better part of myself—the part that says "No matter what, I'm here for you." What I know for sure is that Gayle is a friend I can count on. She has taught me the joy of having, and being, a true friend.

Getting *three new pups* at the same time wasn't the smartest decision I ever made. I acted on impulse, charmed by their cute little faces, intoxicated by that sweet puppy breath and the underbite on Puppy No. 3 (Layla).

Then I spent weeks getting up at all hours of the night with them. I picked up pounds of poop and spent hours puppy training so they would have good manners.

It was a *lot* of work. I was sleep deprived—and constantly frazzled from trying to keep three at a time from destroying all my worldly goods. Whoa, did I gain a big new respect for mothers of real babies!

All this puppy love was starting to get on my nerves, so I had to make a paradigm shift. One day while walking them, I stood and watched them frolic—and I do mean frolic: rolling, tumbling, chasing, laughing (yes, dogs laugh), and leaping like bunnies. They were having so much fun, and seeing them that way made my whole body sigh, relax, and smile. New life discovering a field of grass for the first time: What a wonder!

We all get the opportunity to feel wonder every day, but we've been lulled into numbness. Have you ever driven home from work, opened your front door, and asked yourself how you got there?

I know for sure that I don't want to live a shut-down life—desensitized to feeling and seeing. I want every day to be a fresh start on expanding what is possible. On experiencing joy on every level.

I love *building a fire* in the fireplace. What a sense of accomplishment it is to stack the wood exactly right (pyramid-style) and have the flames shoot up without using a starter log! I don't know why that's so rewarding for me, but it is—as a young girl, I dreamed of being a Girl Scout but could never afford the uniform.

A fire is even better when it's pouring rain outside. And it's absolutely the best when I've finished my work, checked my e-mail, unplugged, and am ready to read.

Everything I do all day, I do in preparation for my reading time. Give me a great novel or memoir, some tea, and a cozy spot to curl up in, and I'm in heaven. I love to live in another person's thoughts; I marvel at the bonds I feel with people who come alive on the page, regardless of how different their circumstances might be from mine. I not only feel I know these people, but I also recognize more of myself. Insight, information, knowledge, inspiration, power: All that and more can come through a good book.

I can't imagine where I'd be or who I'd be without the essential tool of reading. I for sure wouldn't have gotten my first job in radio at the age of 16. I was touring the radio station WVOL in Nashville when the DJ asked, "Do you want to hear how your voice sounds on tape?" and handed me a piece of news copy and a microphone. "You oughta hear this girl!" he exclaimed to his boss. There began my broadcasting career—shortly thereafter, the station hired me to read the news on the air. After years of reciting poetry to whomever would listen and reading everything I could get my hands on, someone was going to pay me to do what I loved—read out loud.

Books, for me, used to be a way to escape. I now consider reading a good book a sacred indulgence, a chance to be any place I choose. It is my absolute favorite way to spend time. What I know for sure is that reading opens you up. It exposes you and gives you access to anything your mind can hold. What I love most about reading: It gives you the ability to reach higher ground. And keep climbing.

My *primary and most* essential goal in life is to remain connected to the world of spirit. Everything else will take care of itself—this I know for sure. And my number-one spiritual practice is trying to live in the present moment . . . to resist projecting into the future, or lamenting past mistakes . . . to feel the real power of now. That, my friends, is the secret to a joyful life.

If everybody remembered to live this way (as children do when they first arrive on this planet; it's what we hardened souls call innocence), we'd transform the world. Playing, laughing, feeling joy.

My favorite Bible verse, which I have loved since I was an eight-year-old girl, is Psalms 37:4. "Delight thyself in the Lord, and He will give you the desires of your heart." This has been my mantra through all my experience. Delight in the Lord—in goodness, kindness, compassion, love—and see what happens.

I dare you.

Resilience

———— ❧ ————

"Barn's burnt down / Now I can see the moon."

—Mizuta Masahide
(seventeenth-century Japanese poet)

No *matter who we are* or where we come from, we all have our own journey. Mine began one April afternoon in 1953, in rural Mississippi, where I was conceived out of wedlock by Vernon Winfrey and Vernita Lee. Their onetime union that day, not at all a romance, brought about an unwanted pregnancy, and my mother concealed her condition until the day I was born—so no one was prepared for my arrival. There were no baby showers, none of the anticipation or delight that I see in the faces of expectant friends who rub their swollen stomachs with reverence. My birth was marked by regret, hiding, and shame.

When the author and counselor John Bradshaw, who pioneered the concept of the inner child, appeared on *The Oprah Winfrey Show* in 1991, he took my audience and me through a profound exercise. He asked us to close our eyes and go back to the home we grew up in, to visualize the house itself. Come closer, he said. Look inside the window and find yourself inside. What do you see? And more important, what do you feel? For me it was an overwhelmingly sad yet powerful exercise. What I felt at almost every stage of my development was lonely. Not alone—because there were always people around—but I knew that my soul's survival depended on me. I felt I would have to fend for myself.

As a girl, I used to love when company would come to my grandmother's house after church. When they left, I dreaded being alone with my grandfather, who was senile, and my grandmother, who was often exhausted and impatient. I was the only child for miles around, so I had to learn to be with myself. I invented new ways to be solitary. I had books and homemade dolls and chores and farm animals I often named and talked to. I'm sure that all that time alone was critical in defining the adult I would become.

Looking back through John Bradshaw's window into my life, I was sad that the people closest to me didn't seem to realize what a sweet-spirited little girl I was. But I also felt strengthened, seeing it for myself.

Like me, you might have experienced things that caused you to deem yourself unworthy. I know for sure that healing the wounds of the past is one of the biggest and most worthwhile challenges of life. It's important to know when and how you were programmed, so you can change the program. And doing so is your responsibility, no one else's. There is one irrefutable law of the universe: We are each responsible for our own life.

If you're holding anyone else accountable for your happiness, you're wasting your time. You must be fearless enough to give yourself the love you didn't receive. Begin noticing how every day brings a new opportunity for your growth. How buried disagreements with your mother show up in arguments with your spouse. How unconscious feelings of unworthiness appear in everything you do (and don't do). All these experiences are your life's way of urging you to leave the past behind and make yourself whole. Pay attention. Every choice gives you a chance to pave your own road. Keep moving. Full speed ahead.

Every *challenge we take* on has the power to knock us to our knees. But what's even more disconcerting than the jolt itself is our fear that we won't withstand it. When we feel the ground beneath us shifting, we panic. We forget everything we know and allow fear to freeze us. Just the thought of what could happen is enough to throw us off balance.

What I know for sure is that the only way to endure the quake is to adjust your stance. You can't avoid the daily tremors. They come with being alive. But I believe these experiences are gifts that force us to step to the right or left in search of a new center of gravity. Don't fight them. Let them help you adjust your footing.

Balance lives in the present. When you feel the earth moving, bring yourself back to the now. You'll handle whatever shake-up the next moment brings when you get to it. In *this* moment, you're still breathing. In *this* moment, you've survived. In *this* moment, you're finding a way to step onto higher ground.

F or years, I had a secret that almost no one knew. Even Gayle, who knew everything about me, wasn't aware of it until several years into our friendship. The same is true for Stedman. I hid it until I felt safe enough to share: the years I was sexually abused, from age 10 to 14, my resulting promiscuity, and finally, at 14, my becoming pregnant. I was so ashamed, I hid the pregnancy until my doctor noticed my swollen ankles and belly. I gave birth in 1968; the baby died in the hospital weeks later.

I went back to school and told no one. My fear was that if I were found out, I would be expelled. So I carried the secret into my future, always afraid that if anyone discovered what had happened, they, too, would expel me from their lives. Even when I found the courage to publicly reveal the abuse, I still carried the shame and kept the pregnancy a secret.

When a family member who has since died leaked this story to the tabloids, everything changed. I felt devastated.

Wounded. Betrayed. How could this person do this to me? I cried and cried. I remember Stedman coming into the bedroom that Sunday afternoon, the room darkened from the closed curtains. Standing before me, looking like he, too, had shed tears, he said, "I'm so sorry. You don't deserve this."

When I dragged myself from bed for work that Monday morning after the news broke, I felt beaten and scared. I imagined that every person on the street was going to point their finger at me and scream, "Pregnant at fourteen, you wicked girl . . . expelled!" No one said a word, though—not strangers, not the people I knew. I was shocked. Nobody treated me differently. For decades, I had been expecting a reaction that never came.

I've since been betrayed by others—but although it's a kick in the gut, it doesn't make me cry or take to my bed anymore. I try never to forget the words of Isaiah 54:17: "No weapon formed against you shall prosper." Every difficult moment has its silver lining, and I soon realized that having the secret out was liberating. Not until then could I begin repairing the damage done to my spirit as a young girl. I realized that all those years, I had been blaming myself. What I learned for sure was that holding the shame was the greatest burden of all. When you have nothing to be ashamed of, when you know who you are and what you stand for, you stand in wisdom.

Whenever I'm faced with a difficult decision, I ask myself: What would I do if I weren't afraid of making a mistake, feeling rejected, looking foolish, or being alone? I know for sure that when you remove the fear, the answer you've been searching for comes into focus. And as you walk into what you fear, *you* should know for sure that your deepest struggle can, if you're willing and open, produce your greatest strength.

H*ave you ever come* across an old picture and been instantly transported back in time—to the point where you can feel the clothes you were wearing?

There's a photo of me at 21 years old that gives me exactly this feeling. The skirt I was wearing cost $40—more than I'd ever spent on a single item of clothing—but I was willing to do it for my first major celebrity interview: Jesse Jackson. He was speaking at a local high school, telling students, "Down with dope, up with hope!"—and I had been assigned to cover him. My news director didn't think the event was worth our time, but I'd insisted (okay, pleaded), assuring him I could come back with a piece worthy of the six o'clock news. And I did.

I had a fondness for telling other people's stories, extracting the truth of their experience and distilling it into wisdom that could inform, inspire, or benefit someone else. Still, I was uncertain about what to say to Jackson, or how to say it.

If I knew then what I know now, I would never have wasted even a single minute doubting my path.

Because when it comes to matters of the heart, emotion, connection, and speaking in front of large audiences, I thrive. Something happens between me and whomever I'm engaged with: I can feel them and sense that they are vibing right back with me. That's because I know for sure that anything I've been through or felt, they have, too, and probably more so. The great connection I feel with everyone I speak to stems from being aware that we are all on the same path, all of us wanting the same things: love, joy, and acknowledgment.

No matter what challenge you may be facing, you must remember that while the canvas of your life is painted with daily experiences, behaviors, reactions, and emotions, *you're* the one controlling the brush. If I had known this at 21, I could have saved myself a lot of heartache and self-doubt. It would have been a revelation to understand that we are all the artists of our own lives—and that we can use as many colors and brushstrokes as we like.

I *have always prided* myself on my independence, my integrity, my support of others. But there's a thin line between pride and ego. And I've learned that sometimes you have to step out of your ego to recognize the truth. So when life gets difficult, I've found that the best thing to do is ask myself a simple question: *What is this here to teach me?*

I remember back in 1988, when I first took ownership of the *Oprah* show, I had to buy a studio and hire all the producers. There were a million things I didn't know. I made a lot of mistakes during those early years (including one so big we had a priest come in to cleanse the studio afterward). Fortunately for me, I wasn't so well-known back then. I could learn a lesson, and grow from it, privately.

Today, part of the price of success is that my lessons are public. If I stumble, people know, and some days the pressure of that reality makes me want to scream. But one thing I know for sure: I am not a screamer. I can count on one hand the number of times in my life—four—when I've actually raised my voice at someone.

So when I feel overwhelmed, I usually go to a quiet place. A bathroom stall works wonders. I close my eyes, turn inward, and breathe until I can sense the still, small space inside me that is the same as the stillness in you, and in the trees, and in all things. I breathe until I can feel this space expand and fill me. And I always end up doing the exact opposite of screaming: I smile at the wonder of it all.

I mean, how amazing is it that I, a woman born and raised in Mississippi when it was an apartheid state, who grew up having to go into town even to watch TV—we certainly didn't have one at home—am where I am today?

Wherever you are in your journey, I hope you, too, will keep encountering challenges. It is a blessing to be able to survive them, to be able to keep putting one foot in front of the other—to be in a position to make the climb up life's mountain, knowing that the summit still lies ahead. And every experience is a valuable teacher.

We all have *stand-down* moments that require us to stand up, in the center of ourselves, and know who we are. When your marriage falls apart, when a job that defined you is gone, when the people you'd counted on turn their backs on you, there's no question that changing the way you think about your situation is the key to improving it. I know for sure that all of our hurdles have meaning. And being open to learning from those challenges is the difference between succeeding and getting stuck.

As I get older, I can feel my body making a shift. No matter how I try, I can't run as fast as I could before, but to tell you the truth, I don't really care to. Everything's shifting: breasts and knees and attitude. I marvel at my own sense of calm now. Events that used to leave me reeling, with my head in a bag of chips, no longer even faze me. Even better, I'm privy to insights about myself that only a lifetime of learning can bring.

I've said that I always knew I was exactly where I was meant to be when I was standing on the stage talking to viewers around the world. That was truly my sweet spot. But the universe is full of surprises. Because I'm learning that where sweet spots are concerned, we're not limited to just one. At different times in our journeys, if we're paying attention, we get to sing the song we're meant to sing in the perfect key of life. Everything we've ever done and all we're meant to do comes together in harmony with who we are. When that happens, we feel the truest expression of ourselves.

I feel myself heading there now, and it's my wish for you, too.

One of my greatest lessons has been to fully understand that what looks like a dark patch in the quest for success is the universe pointing you in a new direction. Anything can be a miracle, a blessing, an opportunity if you choose to see it that way. Had I not been demoted from my six o'clock anchor post in Baltimore back in 1977, the talk show gig would never have happened when it did.

When you can see obstacles for what they are, you never lose faith in the path it takes to get you where you want to go. Because this I know for sure: Who you're meant to be evolves from where you are right now. So learning to appreciate your lessons, mistakes, and setbacks as stepping-stones to the future is a clear sign you're moving in the right direction.

D uring *difficult times* I often turn to a gospel song called "Stand." In it, songwriter Donnie McClurkin sings, "What do you do when you've done all you can, and it seems like it's never enough? What do you give when you've given your all, and it seems like you can't make it through?" The answer lies in McClurkin's simple refrain: "You just stand."

That's where strength comes from—our ability to face resistance and walk through it. It's not that people who persevere don't ever feel doubt, fear, and exhaustion. They do. But in the toughest moments, we can have faith that if we take just one step more than we feel we're capable of, if we draw on the incredible resolve every human being possesses, we'll learn some of the most profound lessons life has to offer.

What I know for sure is that there is no strength without challenge, adversity, resistance, and often pain. The problems that make you want to throw up your hands and holler "Mercy!" will build your tenacity, courage, discipline, and determination.

I've learned to rely on the strength I inherited from all those who came before me—the grandmothers, sisters, aunts, and brothers who were tested with unimaginable hardships and still survived. "I go forth alone, and stand as ten thousand," Maya Angelou proclaimed in her poem "Our Grandmothers." When I move through the world, I bring all my history with me—all the people who paved the way for me are part of who I am.

Think back for a moment on your *own* history—not just where you were born or where you grew up, but the circumstances that contributed to your being right here, right now. What were the moments along the way that wounded or scared you? Chances are, you've had a few. But here's what's remarkable: You are still here, still standing.

Connection

---❦---

"Love is the essential existential fact. It is our ultimate reality and our purpose on earth."

—Marianne Williamson

T*alking with thousands* of people over the years has shown me that there's one desire we all share: We want to feel valued. Whether you're a mother in Topeka or a businesswoman in Philadelphia, each of us, at our core, longs to be loved, needed, understood, affirmed—to have intimate connections that leave us feeling more alive and human.

I once filmed a show in which I interviewed seven men of different ages and backgrounds, all of whom had one thing in common: They had cheated on their wives. It was one of the most interesting, candid conversations I've ever had, and a huge aha moment for me. I realized that the yearning to feel heard, needed, and important is so strong in all of us that we seek that validation in whatever form we can get it. For a lot of people—men and women—having an affair is an affirmation that *I'm really okay*. One of the men I interviewed, who'd been married 18 years and thought he had a moral code that would withstand flirtatious temptations, said about his mistress, "There wasn't anything special about her. But she listened, was interested, and made me feel special." That's the key, I thought—we all want to feel like we matter to somebody.

As a girl growing up shuffled between Mississippi, Nashville, and Milwaukee, I didn't feel loved. I thought I could make people approve of me by becoming an achiever. Then, in my twenties, I based my worth on whether a man would love me. I remember once even throwing a boyfriend's keys down the toilet to keep him from walking out on me! I was no different from a physically abused woman. I wasn't getting slapped upside the head every night, but because my wings were clipped I couldn't soar. I had so much going for me, but without a man I thought I was nothing. Not until years later did I understand that the love and approval I craved could not be found outside myself.

What I know for sure is that a lack of intimacy is not distance from someone else; it is disregard for yourself. It's true that we all need the kind of relationships that enrich and sustain us. But it's also true that if you're looking for someone to heal and complete you—to shush that voice inside you that has always whispered *You're not worth anything*—you are wasting your time. Why? Because if you don't already know that you have worth, there's nothing your friends, your family, or your mate can say that will completely convince you of that. The Creator has given you full responsibility for your life, and with that responsibility comes an amazing privilege—the power to give yourself the love, affection, and intimacy you may not have received as a child. You are the one best mother, father, sister, friend, cousin, and lover you will ever have.

Right now you're one choice away from seeing yourself as someone whose life has inherent significance—so choose to see it that way. You don't have to spend one more second focusing on a past deprived of the affirmation you should have gotten from your parents. Yes, you did deserve that love, but it's up to you now to bestow it upon yourself and move forward. Stop waiting for your husband to say "I appreciate you," your kids to tell you what a great mother you are, a man to whisk you away and marry you, or your best friend to assure you that you're worth a darn. Look inward—the loving begins with you.

T*he key to any* relationship is communication. And I've always thought that communication is like a dance. One person takes a step forward, the other takes a step back. Even a single misstep can land both people on the floor in a tangle of confusion. And when you find yourself in that position—with your spouse, your colleague, your friend, your child—I've found that the best option is always to ask the other person, "What do you really want here?" At first, you might notice a little squirming, a lot of throat clearing, maybe some silence. But if you stay quiet long enough to get the real answer, I guarantee it will be some variation of the following: "I want to know that you value me." Extend a hand of connection and understanding, and offer three of the most important words any of us can ever receive: "I hear you." I know for sure your relationship will be the better for it.

I've never been a social person. I know this may come as a surprise to most people, but ask anyone who knows me well, and they will confirm it's true. I've always kept my downtime for myself, plus a wee circle of friends whom I consider my extended family. I'd been living in Chicago for years before I suddenly realized I could count on one hand—and still have some fingers remaining—the number of times I'd visited friends or met up with someone for dinner or gone out just for fun.

I'd lived in apartments since leaving my dad's house. Apartments where I often didn't take the time to know the person across the hallway, let alone anyone else on my floor. We were all too busy, I told myself. But in 2004, shortly after that realization, I moved to a house—not an apartment, a house—in California, and a whole new world opened up to me. After years spent in the public eye, conversing with some of the world's most fascinating people—I finally became social. For the first time in my adult life, I felt like I was part of a community. Just after

I arrived, as I was pushing my cart down the cereal aisle at Von's, a woman I didn't know stopped me and said, "Welcome to the neighborhood. We all love it here and hope you will, too." She said it with such sincerity that I wanted to weep.

In that moment, I made a conscious decision not to close the gate to my life as I had for so many years living in the city, shutting myself off to even the possibility of a new circle of friends. I now live in a neighborhood where everybody knows me and I know them.

First, Joe and Judy invited me next door for Joe's homemade pizza and said it would be ready in an hour. I hesitated only a moment. I put on my flip-flops, headed over in sweatpants and zero makeup, and ended up staying the afternoon. Chattin' it up at a stranger's house, finding common ground, was brand-new territory for me— bordering on adventurous.

Since then, I've had tea with the Abercrombies, who live three doors down. Been to a backyard barbecue at Bob and Marlene's . . . a pool party at Barry and Jelinda's . . . had watermelon martinis at Julie's . . . took in a rose garden gathering at Sally's. I attended a formal sit-down at Annette and Harold's with more silverware than I could manage, and a rib-cooking contest (which I deserved to win but didn't) at Margo's. I watched the sunset and ate black-eyed peas at the Nicholsons', and attended an all-out feast under the stars with 50 neighbors at the Reitmans'. I knew all but two of them by name. So, yes: I've become *verrrrrry* social.

And because of that, my life has a new, unexpected layer. I thought I was through making friends. But much to my surprise, I've found myself looking forward to hanging out, laughing, connecting with and embracing others as a part of the circle. It's added new meaning to my life, a feeling of community I didn't even know I was missing.

What I know for sure is that everything happens for a reason—and the stranger who approached me in the grocery store with such feeling triggered something: the possibility that I could make this new neighborhood a real home and not just a place to live. I've always known that life is better when you share it. But I now realize it gets even sweeter when you expand the circle.

Let's face it: Love's a subject that's been done and overdone, trivialized and dramatized to the point of mass delusion about what it is and isn't. Most of us can't see it because we have our own preconceived ideas about what it is (it's supposed to knock you off your feet and make you swoon) and how it should appear (in a tall, slim, witty, charming package). So if love doesn't show up wrapped in our personal fantasy, we fail to recognize it.

But this is what I know for sure: Love is all around. It's possible to love and be loved, no matter where you are. Love exists in all forms. Sometimes I walk into my front yard and I can feel all my trees just vibrating love. It is always available for the asking.

I've seen so many women (myself included) dazed by the idea of romance, believing they're not complete unless they find someone to make their lives whole. When you think about it, isn't that a crazy notion? You, alone, make a whole person. And if you feel incomplete, you alone must fill all your empty, shattered spaces with love. As Ralph

Waldo Emerson said, "Nothing can bring you peace but yourself."

I'll never forget the time I was cleaning out a drawer and came across 12 pages that stopped me in my tracks. It was a *looove* letter I'd written but never sent (thank God) to a guy I was dating. I was 29 at the time, desperate and obsessed with this man. It was 12 pages of whinin' and pinin' so pathetic that I didn't recognize myself. And though I've kept my journals since age 15, I held my own burning ceremony for this testament to what I thought was love. I wanted no written record that I was ever that pitiful and disconnected from myself.

I've seen so many women give themselves up for men who clearly didn't give two hoots about them. I've seen so many women settle for crumbs. But now I know that a relationship built on real love feels *good*. It should bring you joy—not just some of the time but most of the time. It should never require losing your voice, your self-respect, or your dignity. And whether you're 25 or 65, it should involve bringing all of who you are to the table—and walking away with even more.

Romantic love is not the only love worth seeking. I've met so many people longing to be in love with somebody, to be rescued from their daily lives and swept into romantic bliss, when all around there are children, neighbors, friends, and strangers also yearning for someone to connect with. Look around and notice—possibility is everywhere.

On the other hand, if you find it a strain to open your heart full-throttle to the Big L, start in first gear: Show compassion, and before long you'll feel yourself shifting to something deeper. Soon, you'll be able to offer others the blessings of understanding, empathy, caring, and—I know for sure—love.

In *times of crisis*, I've always marveled at the way
people reach out with words of encouragement. I've
had moments of real devastation in my life—we all have—
but I've been sustained by the grace and love of friends
who have asked, "Is there anything I can do to help?" not
knowing that they already have, just by asking. People
I've known well and others I've never met have, in tough
moments, built me a bridge of support.

I'll never forget when, after a particularly difficult
setback a few years ago, my friend BeBe Winans stopped
by unexpectedly. "There's something I came to tell you," he
said. And he started singing what he knows is my favorite
spiritual: "I surrender all. I surrender all. All to thee, my
blessed Savior, I surrender all."

I sat silently, closed my eyes, and opened myself to this
gift of love and song. When he finished, I felt a release of
all pressure. I was content to just be. And for the first time
in weeks, I experienced pure peace.

When I opened my eyes and wiped away the tears, BeBe was beaming. He started laughing his *huh, huh, huuuagh* laugh, and gave me a big hug. "Girl," he said, "I just came to remind you, you don't have to carry this load all by yourself."

To know that people care about how you're doing when the doing isn't so good—that's what love is. I feel blessed to know this for sure.

I *thought I knew* a lot about friendship until I spent 11 days traveling across the country in a Chevy Impala with Gayle King. We've been close since we were in our early twenties. We've helped each other through tough times, vacationed together, worked on my magazine together. And still there was more to learn.

On Memorial Day 2006, we set out to "see the U.S.A. in a Chevrolet." Remember that commercial from years ago? Well, I always thought it was a charming idea. When we pulled out of my driveway in California, we were singing the jingle loudly, with vibrato, cracking ourselves up. Three days in, around Holbrook, Arizona, we were mumbling the tune. And by Lamar, Colorado, five days in, we'd stopped singing altogether.

The trip was grueling. Every day, six, then eight, then ten hours with nothing but road stretched ahead. When Gayle drove, she insisted on constant music; I wanted silence. "To be alone with my thoughts" became a running joke. As she sang along boisterously, I realized there wasn't a tune she didn't know. (She called almost everyone her favorite.) This was as nerve-racking for me as the silence was for her when I was behind the wheel. I learned patience. And when patience wore thin, I bought earplugs. Every night, landing in a different hotel, we were exhausted but still able to laugh at ourselves. We laughed at my merging anxiety, interstate anxiety, and passing-another-vehicle anxiety. Oh, and crossing-a-bridge anxiety.

Of course, Gayle will tell you I'm not a great driver. She herself is a masterly driver, taking the curves on the Pennsylvania Turnpike with ease and steadily leading us into New York. Only one glitch: By the time we reached Pennsylvania, her contacts had been in too long and her eyes were tired. We approached the George Washington Bridge, relieved to end the long run of Cheetos and pork rinds from gas stations. Dusk had fallen, and night was approaching fast. Gayle said, "I hate to tell you this, but I can't see."

"What do you mean, you can't see?" I tried to ask calmly.

"All the headlights have halos. Do they have halos to you?"

"Uhhhh, no, they do not. *Can You See the Lines on the Road?*" I was shouting now, envisioning the headline: FRIENDS FINISH JOURNEY IN A CRASH ON GW BRIDGE. There was nowhere to pull over, and cars were speeding by.

"I know this bridge very well," she said. "That's what's saving us. And I have a plan. When we get to the toll, I'm going to pull over and take out my contacts and get my glasses."

The toll was a long way ahead. "What can I do?" I said, near panic. "Do you need me to steer for you?"

"No, I'm going to hug the white lines. Can you take out my contacts and put on my glasses?" she joked. At least I think she was joking.

"That would be dangerous and impossible," I said.

"Then turn up the air, I'm sweatin'," she said.

We both sweated our way to the toll booth—and safely pulled into New York. The crew following us had T-shirts made: I SURVIVED THE ROAD TRIP.

What I know for sure is that if you can survive 11 days in cramped quarters with a friend and come out laughing, your friendship is real.

The story of how my beloved dog Sadie came into my life is one for the ages: At a humane shelter in Chicago, she hugged my shoulder, licked my ear, and whispered, "Please take me with you." I could feel her making a bid for a new life with me.

I felt an instant connection with her. But just to be sure I wasn't caught up in a moment of overwhelming puppy love, Gayle said, "Why don't you wait and see how you feel tomorrow?" So I decided to wait 24 hours. The next day, Chicago had a whiteout blizzard—not a good day to bring a puppy home, I thought. Especially if you live in a high-rise. It's hard to house-train from the seventy-seventh floor even when the sun is shining—puppies need to go outside a *lot* when they're first learning when (and when not) to go.

Nevertheless, Stedman and I donned our winter gear and used our four-wheel-drive to get across town. Just to "have another look," I swore. Miss Sadie, the runt of the litter, spoke to my heart. I love making the underdog a winner.

An hour later we were at Petco, buying a crate and wee-wee pads, collar and leash, puppy food and toys.

The crate started out next to the bed. And still she cried. We moved the crate up onto the bed, right in the center, so she had a full view of me—I wanted to do anything I could to help her avoid separation anxiety on her first night away from the litter. And yet there was more whimpering and whining. Then full-blown yelping. So I took her out of the crate and let her sleep on my pillow. I know that's no way to train a dog. But I did it anyway—to the point where Sadie thought *I* was her littermate. By the time I woke up in the morning, she had nuzzled her way to my shoulder, which was her most comfortable sleeping position.

Five days after bringing her home, I lost track of good sense and let myself get talked into adopting her brother Ivan. For 24 hours, life was grand: Ivan was Sadie's playmate, and I didn't have to be. (It was nice to get some relief from games of fetch and rubber squeezy bunnies.)

Ivan had one full day of romping in the sun with Sadie and my two golden retrievers, Luke and Layla. Then he refused dinner. And then the diarrhea started, followed by vomiting and more diarrhea. That was on Saturday. By Monday night, we knew he had the dreaded parvovirus.

I'd been through parvo 13 years before, with my brown cocker, Solomon. It nearly killed him. He stayed in the veterinary hospital for 20 days. He was more than a year old when he got it. Ivan was only 11 weeks. His young immune system wasn't strong enough to overcome it. Four days after we took Ivan to the emergency clinic, he died.

That morning, Sadie refused to eat. Even though she had tested negative before, I knew she had parvo, too.

So began the ordeal of trying to save her. Plasma transfusions. Antibiotics. Probiotics. And daily visits. I wish for every citizen of this country the kind of health care and treatment this little dog received. The first four days, she got increasingly worse. At one point I told the vet, "I'm prepared to let her go. She shouldn't have to fight this hard."

But fight she did. By the next day her white blood cell count started to improve, and two days later she was happily eating bits of chicken.

Shortly afterward Sadie came home, skinny and frail but ready to start life anew. She eventually recovered fully.

During the time she and Ivan spent in the hospital, I was worried and restless and got little sleep—the same as it would have been with any family member. Which is what I know for sure pets represent in our lives: a connection to caring that's unconditional. And reciprocal.

Puppy love. Nothing like it.

When *you make loving* others the story of your life, there's never a final chapter, because the legacy continues. You lend your light to one person, and he or she shines it on another and another and another. And I know for sure that in the final analysis of our lives—when the to-do lists are no more, when the frenzy is finished, when our e-mail inboxes are empty—the only thing that will have any lasting value is whether we've loved others and whether they've loved us.

Gratitude

"*If the only prayer you ever say in your entire life is
'Thank you,' it will be enough.*"

—Meister Eckhart

For years I've been advocating the power and pleasure of being grateful. I kept a gratitude journal for a full decade without fail—and urged everyone I knew to do the same. Then life got busy. My schedule overwhelmed me. I still opened my journal some nights, but my ritual of writing down five things I was grateful for every day started slipping away.

Here's what I was grateful for on October 12, 1996:

1. A run around Florida's Fisher Island with a slight breeze that kept me cool.

2. Eating cold melon on a bench in the sun.
3. A long and hilarious chat with Gayle about her blind date with Mr. Potato Head.
4. Sorbet in a cone, so sweet that I licked my finger.
5. Maya Angelou calling to read me a new poem.

A few years ago, when I came across that journal entry, I wondered why I no longer felt the joy of simple moments. Since 1996, I had accumulated more wealth, more responsibility, more possessions; everything, it seemed, had grown exponentially—except my happiness. How had I, with all my options and opportunities, become one of those people who never have time to feel delight? I was stretched in so many directions, I wasn't feeling much of anything. Too busy doing.

But the truth is, I was busy in 1996, too. I just made gratitude a daily priority. I went through the day looking for things to be grateful for, and something always showed up.

Sometimes we get so focused on the difficulty of our climb that we lose sight of being grateful for simply having a mountain *to* climb.

My life is still crazy busy. Today, though, I'm continuously grateful for having the stamina to keep going. And I'm back to journaling (electronically, this time around). Whenever there's a grateful moment, I note it. I know for sure that appreciating whatever shows up for you in life changes your whole world. You radiate and generate more goodness for yourself when you're aware of all you have and not focusing on your have-nots.

I know for sure: If you make time for a little gratitude every day, you'll be amazed by the results.

S ay thank-you!" Many years ago, those words from Maya Angelou turned my life around. I was on the phone with her, sitting in my bathroom with the door closed and the toilet lid down, weeping so uncontrollably that I was incoherent.

"Stop it!" Maya chided. "Stop it right now and say thank-you!"

"But you—you don't understand," I sobbed. To this day, I can't remember what it was that had me so far gone, which only proves the point Maya was trying to make.

"I do understand," she told me. "I want to hear you say it now. Out loud. 'Thank you.'"

Tentatively, I repeated it: "Thank you." And then snuffled some more. "But what am I saying thank-you for?"

"You're saying thank-you," Maya said, "because your faith is so strong that you don't doubt that whatever the problem, you'll get through it. You're saying thank-you because you know that even in the eye of the storm, God has put a rainbow in the clouds. You're saying thank-you because you know there's no problem created that can compare to the Creator of all things. Say thank-you!"

So I did—and still do.

Being grateful all the time isn't easy. But it's when you feel least thankful that you are most in need of what gratitude can give you: perspective. Gratitude can transform any situation. It alters your vibration, moving you from negative energy to positive. It's the quickest, easiest, most powerful way to effect change in your life—this I know for sure.

Here's the gift of gratitude: In order to feel it, your ego has to take a backseat. What shows up in its place is greater compassion and understanding. Instead of being frustrated, you choose appreciation. And the more grateful you become, the more you have to be grateful for.

Maya Angelou was so right. Whatever you're going through, you will do just that: go through it. It will pass. So say thank-you now. Because you know the rainbow is coming.

The *amount of time* and energy I've spent thinking about what my next meal will be is incalculable: what to eat, what I just ate, how many calories or grams of fat it contains, how much exercise I'll need to do to burn it off, what if I don't work out, how long will it take to manifest as extra pounds, and on and on. Food has been on my mind a lot over the years.

I still have the check I wrote to my first diet doctor—Baltimore, 1977. I was 23 years old, 148 pounds, a size 8, and I thought I was fat. The doctor put me on a 1,200-calorie regimen, and in less than two weeks I had lost 10 pounds. Two months later, I'd regained 12. Thus began the cycle of discontent, the struggle with my body. With myself.

I joined the dieting brigade—signing on for the Beverly Hills, Atkins, Scarsdale, Cabbage Soup, and even the Banana, Hot Dog, and Egg diets. (You think I'm kidding. I wish.) What I didn't know is that with each diet, I was starving my muscles, slowing my metabolism, and setting myself up to gain even more weight. Around 1995, after almost two decades of yo-yoing, I finally realized that being grateful for my body, whatever shape it was in, was the key to giving more love to myself.

But although I made that connection intellectually, living it was a different story. It wasn't until about six years later, after six months of unexplained heart palpitations, that I finally got it. On December 19, 2001, I wrote in my journal: "One thing is for sure—having palpitations at night makes me more aware of being happy to awaken in the morning, more grateful for each day." I stopped taking my heart for granted and began thanking it for every beat it had ever given me. I marveled at the wonder of it: In 47 years, I'd never consciously given a thought to what my heart does, feeding oxygen to my lungs, liver, pancreas, even my brain, one beat at a time.

For so many years, I had let my heart down by not giving it the support it needed. Overeating. Overstressing. Overdoing. No wonder when I lay down at night it couldn't stop racing. I believe everything that happens in our lives has meaning, that each experience brings a message, if we're willing to hear it. So what was my speeding heart trying to tell me? I still didn't know the answer. Yet simply asking the question caused me to look at my body and how I had failed to honor it. How every diet I had ever been on was because I wanted to fit into something—or just fit in. Taking care of my heart, the life force of my body, had never been my priority.

I sat up in bed one crisp, sunny morning and made a vow to love my heart. To treat it with respect. To feed and nurture it. To work it out and then let it rest. And then one night when I was getting out of the tub, I glanced in the full-length mirror. For the first time, I didn't launch into my self-criticism. I actually felt a warming sense of gratitude for what I saw. My hair braided, not a stitch of makeup on, face clean. Eyes bright, alive. Shoulders and neck strong and firm. I was thankful for the body I lived in.

I did a head-to-toe assessment, and though there was plenty of room for improvement, I no longer hated any part of myself, even the cellulite. I thought, *This is the body you've been given—love what you've got.* So I started truly loving the face I was born with; the lines I had under my eyes at age 2 have gotten deeper, but they're my lines. The broad nose I tried to lift, when I was 8, by sleeping with a clothespin and two cotton balls on the sides, is the nose

I've grown into. The full lips I used to pull in when smiling are the lips I've used to speak to millions of people every day—my lips need to be full.

In that moment, as I stood before the mirror, I had my own "spiritual transformation/a root revival of love," which Carolyn M. Rodgers writes of in one of my favorite poems, "Some Me of Beauty."

What I know for sure: There is no need to struggle with your body when you can make a loving and grateful peace with it.

I *live in the space* of thankfulness—and for that, I have been rewarded a million times over. I started out giving thanks for small things, and the more thankful I became, the more my bounty increased. That's because—for sure—what you focus on expands. When you focus on the goodness in your life, you create more of it.

We've all heard that it's more blessed to give than to receive. Well, I know for sure that it's also a lot more fun. Nothing makes me happier than a gift well given and joyfully received.

I can honestly say that every gift I've ever given has brought at least as much happiness to me as it has to the person I've given it to. I give as I feel. Throughout the year, that may mean mailing a handwritten note to someone who didn't expect it. Or sending a great new lotion I just discovered, or delivering a book of poetry with a pretty bow. It doesn't matter what the thing is; what matters is how much of yourself goes into the giving, so that when the gift is gone, the spirit of you lingers.

My friend Geneviève once left a white bowl of bright yellow lemons with their stems and leaves, freshly picked from her backyard and tied with a green ribbon, on my front doorstep with a note that said "Good morning." The whole presentation was so beautiful in its simplicity that long after the lemons shriveled, I felt the spirit of the gift every time I passed the place where the bowl had been set. I now keep a bowl filled with lemons to remind me of that "Good morning."

You may have heard about the time I gave away a bunch of cars on my show. Pontiac G6s. It was the most fun I'd ever had on TV. But before the great giveaway, I sat meditating in my darkened closet, trying to stay in the moment and not get anxious about the big surprise that was to come. It was important to me to fill the audience with people who really needed new cars, so that all the excitement would have meaning. I wanted the gift to be about the essence of sharing what you have. I prayed for that, sitting in the dark amongst my shoes and handbags. Then I walked downstairs to the studio, and my prayers were answered.

I'm a country girl at heart, having grown up in rural Mississippi—where if you didn't grow it or raise it (as in hogs and chickens), you didn't eat it. Helping my grandmother pull turnip greens from the garden, then sitting on the porch snapping beans and shelling peas, was a routine I took for granted.

Today my favorite day of the week in spring, summer, and fall is harvest day. We go out to the garden to gather artichokes, spinach, squash, green beans, corn, tomatoes, and lettuce, along with basketfuls of fresh herbs, onions, and garlic. The bounty of it gives my heart a thrill!

I'm in awe every time: By planting so little, you can reap so much. In fact, my problem is volume. I can't eat it all, but I don't want to throw away anything that I've watched grow; discarding food you've grown from seed feels like throwing away a gift. I readily share with my neighbors, and still there's always more growing.

All good food comes from the earth. And whether you get that food from a farmers' market, your local grocer, or your own backyard, this I know for sure: The pure joy of eating well is worth savoring.

I once sliced a fresh peach that was so sweet, so succulent, so divinely peachy that even as I was eating it I thought, *There are no words to adequately describe this peach—one has to taste it to understand the true definition of peachiness.* I closed my eyes, the better to enjoy the flavor. But even that wasn't enough, so I saved the last two bites to share with Stedman, to see if he affirmed my assessment of best peach ever. He took the first bite and said, "Mmm, mmm, mmm . . . this peach reminds me of childhood." And so that small thing got bigger, as all things do when shared in a spirit of appreciation.

I *still remember* the first time I stepped outside my box of giving only to family and friends, and did something significant for someone I didn't know. I was a reporter in Baltimore and had covered a story about a young mother and her children, who had fallen on hard times. I'll never forget going back to their home and taking the whole family to a mall to buy winter coats. They so appreciated the gesture, and I learned how good it feels to do something unexpected for someone in need.

Since that time in the late 1970s, I've been blessed with the ability to give truly great gifts—everything from cashmere sheets to college educations. I've given homes. Cars. Trips around the world. The services of a wonderful nanny. But the best gift anyone can give, I believe, is the gift of themselves.

At my fiftieth-birthday luncheon, every woman in attendance wrote a note sharing what our friendship meant to her. All the notes were placed in a silver box. That box still has a treasured space on my nightstand; on days when I'm feeling less than joyful, I'll pull out a note and let it lift me back up.

About a year later I hosted a weekend of festivities to honor 18 magnificent bridge-building, boundary-breaking women and a few dozen of the younger women whose way they had paved. I called it the Legends Ball, and after it was over, I received thank-you letters from all the "young'uns" in attendance. The letters were calligraphed and bound together in a book. They are among my most valued possessions. And they inspired me recently, when a friend was going through a rough time: I called all of *her* friends and asked them to write her love notes, which I then had bound into a book.

I gave to someone else, in the same way that someone had given to me. And I know for sure that's what we're here to do: Keep the giving going.

The table next to me was making a lot of noise, celebrating a special occasion—five waiters singing "Happy birrrrrthday, dear Marilyn . . . " Our side of the room applauded as Marilyn blew out the single candle on the chocolate cupcake she'd been presented with. Someone asked if I'd take a picture with the group.

"Sure," I said, and casually asked, "How old is Marilyn?" to no one in particular.

The whole table laughed nervously. One person said in mock outrage, "I can't believe you're asking that!"

Marilyn ducked her head modestly and told me, "I dare not say."

I was at first amused, then taken aback. "You want a picture honoring your birthday, but you don't want to say how old you are?"

"Well, I don't want to say it out loud. I've been a wreck for weeks knowing this day was coming. It just makes me sick to think about it."

"It makes you sick to think that you've marked another

year, that every worry, every strife, every challenge, every delight, every breath every day was leading to this moment, and now you made it and you're celebrating it—with one little candle—and denying it at the same time?"

"I'm not denying it," she said. "I just don't want to be forty-three."

I gasped in mock horror. "You're *forty-three*? Oh my, I see why you wouldn't want anyone to know that." Everyone laughed that nervous laughter again.

We took the picture, but I didn't stop thinking about Marilyn and her friends.

I also thought about Don Miguel Ruiz, author of one of my favorite books, *The Four Agreements*. According to Don Miguel, "Ninety-five percent of the beliefs we have stored in our minds are nothing but lies, and we suffer because we believe all these lies."

One of these lies that we believe and practice and reinforce is that getting older means getting uglier. We then judge ourselves and others, trying to hold on to the way we were.

This is why, over the years, I have made it a point to

ask women how they feel about aging. I've asked everyone from Bo Derek to Barbra Streisand.

Ali MacGraw told me, "The message women my age send to terrified thirty- and forty-year-old women is that 'it's almost over.' What a gyp."

Beverly Johnson said, "Why am I trying to keep this teenage body when I'm not a teenager and everybody knows it? That was an epiphany for me."

And Cybill Shepherd's honesty offered terrific insight: "I had a great fear, as I grew older, that I would not be valued anymore."

If you're blessed enough to grow older, which is how I look at aging (I think often of all the angels of 9/11 who won't get there), there's so much wisdom to be gained from people who are celebrating the process with vibrancy and vigor and grace.

I've had wonderful mentors in this regard. Maya Angelou, doing speaking tours in her mid-eighties. Quincy Jones, always off in some far-flung part of the world creating new projects. Sidney Poitier, epitomizing who and what I want to be if I'm fortunate to live so long—reading everything he can get his hands on, even writing his first novel at age 85, continuously expanding his fields of knowledge.

For sure we live in a youth-obsessed culture that is constantly trying to tell us that if we're not young and glowing and "hot," we don't matter. But I refuse to buy into such a distorted view of reality. And I would never lie about or deny my age. To do so is to contribute to a sickness pervading our society—the sickness of wanting to be what you're not.

I know for sure that only by owning who and what you are can you step into the fullness of life. I feel sorry for anyone who buys into the myth that you can be what you once were. The way to your best life isn't denial. It's owning every moment and staking a claim to the here and now.

You're not the same woman you were a decade ago; if you're lucky, you're not the same woman you were last year. The whole point of aging, as I see it, is change. If we let them, our experiences can keep teaching us about ourselves. I celebrate that. Honor it. Hold it in reverence. And I'm grateful for every age I'm blessed to become.

I never *foresaw* doing the *Oprah* show for 25 years. Twelve years in, I was already thinking about bringing it to a close. I didn't want to be the girl who stayed too long at the party. I dreaded the thought of overstaying my welcome.

Then I did the movie *Beloved*, portraying a former slave who experiences newfound freedom. That role changed the way I looked at my work. How dare I, who'd been given opportunities unimagined by my ancestors, even think of being tired enough to quit? So I renewed my contract for another four years. Then another two.

At the 20-year mark, I was almost certain that the time was finally right to call it a day. That's when I received an e-mail from Mattie Stepanek.

Mattie was a 12-year-old boy with a rare form of muscular dystrophy who had appeared on my show to read his poetry and became an instant, dear friend. We exchanged e-mails often and talked on the phone when we could. He made me laugh. And sometimes cry. But most often he made me feel more human and present and able to appreciate even the smallest things.

Mattie suffered so much in his young life, going into and out of the hospital, yet hardly ever complained. When he spoke, I listened. And in May 2003, as I was in the throes of deciding whether to bring the show to an end, he was a singular force in changing my mind. Here's the letter he wrote me:

Dear Oprah,

Hello, it's me, Mattie . . . your guy. I am praying and hoping to go home around Memorial Day. It's not a guarantee, so I am not telling a lot of people. It seems that every time I try to go home, something else goes wrong. The doctors are not able to "fix" me, but they agree with me going home. And don't worry, I am not "going home to die" or anything like that. I am going home because they can't do anything else here, and if I heal, it's because I am meant to heal, and if I don't, then my message is out there and it's time for me to go to Heaven. I personally am hoping that my message still needs me to be the messenger a while longer, but that's really in God's hands. But anyway . . . I am only

needing blood transfusions about once a week now, so that
is better. And it sounds weird, but I think it's really cool that
I have blood and platelets from so many people. Makes me
related to the world in some way, which is a proud thing to be.

I know that you are planning to retire your show on its
20th anniversary. It is my opinion that you should wait to stop
your daytime show on its 25th anniversary. Let me explain
why. Twenty-five makes more sense to me, partially because
I am a bit OCD and 25 is a perfect number. It's a perfect
square, and symbolizes a quarter of something, not just a fifth
like the number 20. Also, when I think of the number 25,
especially for retiring or completion, for some reason my mind
is filled with bright colors and the rejuvenation of life. I know
that sounds weird, but it's true. You've already made history in
so many ways, wonderful and beautiful ways, why not make
history bigger by having a show with great dignity that touched
and inspired so many people for a quarter of a century? I'll
let you think on it. And of course it's only my opinion, but I
sometimes get feelings about things, and I have one about this.
I think it's good for the world and good for you.

I love you and you love me,

Mattie

As anyone who knows me knows, I "sometimes get feelings about things," too, and my gut told me to pay attention to this angel boy who I believe was a messenger for our time.

Somehow it was clear to him, back in 2003, that I was neither emotionally nor spiritually prepared to bring that phase of my career to a close.

When I finally was ready for the next chapter, I moved forward with no regrets—only grace and gratitude. And wherever heaven is, I know for sure Mattie is there.

South Dublin Libraries

www.southdublinlibraries.ie

very morning when I open my curtains for that first look at the day, no matter what the day looks like—raining, foggy, overcast, sunny—my heart swells with gratitude. I get another chance.

In the best of times and worst of times, I know for sure, this life is a gift. And I believe that no matter where we live or how we look or what we do for a living, when it comes to what really matters—what makes us laugh and cry, grieve and yearn, delight and rejoice—we share the same heart space. We just fill it with different things. Here are 15 of my favorites:

1. Planting vegetables in my garden.
2. Making blueberry-lemon pancakes on Sunday morning for Stedman. Never fails to delight him—like he's 7 every time.
3. An off-leash romp on the front lawn with all my dogs.

4. A rainy day, a chill in the air, a blazing fire in the fireplace.

5. Picking vegetables from my garden.

6. A great book.

7. Reading in my favorite place on earth: under my oak trees.

8. Cooking vegetables from my garden.

9. Sleeping till my body wants to wake up.

10. Waking up to the real twitter: birds.

11. A workout so strong, my whole body breathes.

12. Eating vegetables from my garden.

13. Being still.

14. Embracing silence.

15. The daily spiritual practice of gratitude. Every day I bless my life by counting my blessings.

Possibility

———— ❧ ————

"Soar, eat ether, see what has never been seen;
depart, be lost,
but climb."

—Edna St. Vincent Millay

How can I *realize* my potential more fully? That's a question I still ask myself, especially when contemplating what's next in my life.

In every job I've taken and every city in which I've lived, I have known that it's time to move on when I've grown as much as I can. Sometimes moving on terrified me. But always it taught me that the true meaning of courage is to be afraid, and then, with your knees knocking, to step out anyway. Making a bold move is the only way to advance toward the grandest vision the universe has for you. If you allow it, fear will completely immobilize you.

And once it has you in its grip, it will fight to keep you from ever becoming your best self.

What I know for sure is this: Whatever you fear most has no power—it is your fear that has the power. The thing itself cannot touch you. But your fear can rob you of your life. Each time you give in to it, you lose strength, while your fear gains it. That's why you must decide that no matter how difficult the path ahead seems, you will push past your anxiety and keep on stepping.

A few years ago, I was writing this question in my journal every day: "What am I afraid of?" Over time I realized that while I had often seemed brave on the outside, I had lived much of my inner life in bondage. I was afraid that others wouldn't like me. I was terrified that if I said no to people, they would reject me. Everything I did, thought, felt, said, or even ate was connected to the fear I carried around with me—and I allowed it to block me from ever knowing who I really was.

Dr. Phil often says you can't change what you don't acknowledge. Before I could challenge my fear and begin changing what I believed about myself, I had to admit that, yes, I had always been afraid—and that my fear was a form of slavery. Author Neale Donald Walsch says, "So long as you're still worried about what others think of you, you are owned by them. Only when you require no approval from outside yourself can you own yourself."

It's true that when you summon the courage to cast a vote for yourself, when you dare to step out, speak up, change yourself, or even simply do something outside of what others call the norm, the results may not always be pleasant. You can expect obstacles. You'll fall down. Others may call you nutty. At times it may feel like the whole world is rising up to tell you who you cannot become and what you cannot do. (It can upset people when you exceed the limited expectations they've always had for you.) And in moments of weakness, your fear and self-doubt may cause you to falter. You may be so exhausted that you want to quit. But the alternatives are even worse: You might find yourself stuck in a miserable rut for years at a time. Or you could spend too many days languishing in regret, always wondering, *What would my life have been like if I hadn't cared so much about what people thought?*

And what if you decided right now that you will stop letting fear block you? What if you learned to live with it, to ride its wave to heights you never knew were possible? You might discover the joy of tuning out what everybody wants for you and finally pay attention to what you need. And learn that, ultimately, you have nothing to prove to anyone but yourself. That is what it truly means to live without fear—and to keep reaching for your best life.

*T*he *true measure of* your courage is not whether you reach your goal—it's whether you decide to get back on your feet no matter how many times you've failed. I know it's not easy, but I also know for sure that having the courage to stand up and pursue your wildest dreams will give you life's richest reward and life's greatest adventure. And what's really wild? Right now, no matter where you are, you are a single choice away from a new beginning.

O ne of my *defining* moments came in the third grade—the day a book report I'd turned in earned my teacher's praise and made my classmates grudgingly whisper, "She thinks she's so smart." For too many years after that, my biggest fear was that others would see me as arrogant. In some ways, even my weight was my apology to the world—my way of saying, "See, I really don't think I'm better than you." The last thing I wanted was for my actions to make me appear full of myself.

Beginning when we are girls, most of us are taught to deflect praise. We apologize for our accomplishments. We try to level the field with our family and friends by downplaying our brilliance. We settle for the passenger's seat when we long to drive. That's why so many of us have been willing to hide our light as adults. Instead of being filled with all the passion and purpose that enable us to offer our best to the world, we empty ourselves in an effort to silence our critics.

The truth is that the naysayers in your life can never be fully satisfied. Whether you hide or shine, they'll always feel threatened because they don't believe *they* are enough. So stop paying attention to them. Every time you suppress some part of yourself or allow others to play you small, you are ignoring the owner's manual your Creator gave you. What I know for sure is this: You are built not to shrink down to less but to blossom into more. To be more splendid. To be more extraordinary. To use every moment to fill yourself up.

I n 1989 *I read* this passage in Gary Zukav's *The Seat of the Soul:*

> Every action, thought, and feeling is motivated by an intention, and that intention is a cause that exists as one with an effect. If we participate in the cause, it is not possible for us not to participate in the effect. In this most profound way, we are held responsible for our every action, thought, and feeling, which is to say, for our every intention. . . . It is, therefore, wise for us to become aware of the many intentions that inform our experience, to sort out which intentions produce which effects, and to choose our intentions according to the effects that we desire to produce.

That was a life-changing paragraph for me. I had recognized for a long time that I was responsible for my life, that every choice produced a consequence. But often the consequences seemed so out of line with my expectations.

That's because I was expecting one thing but intending another. My intention of always trying to please other people, for example, produced an unwanted consequence: I often felt taken advantage of and used, and people came to expect more, more, more from me.

But the principle of intention helped me realize that other people weren't the problem—I was. I decided to do only those things that came from the truth of who I am— and doing only that which pleased me to do for others.

What I know for sure is that whatever your situation is right now, you have played a major role in creating it. With every experience, you build your life, thought by thought, choice by choice. And beneath each of those thoughts and choices lies your deepest intention. That's why, before I make any decision, I ask myself one critical question: *What is my real intention?*

Since reading that passage in *The Seat of the Soul*, I have seen time and again how knowing the answer to that question can be your guiding force. The reverse is also true. When you don't examine your intention, you often end up with consequences that block your progress. Over the years I have witnessed far too many couples who stayed married when they shouldn't have, simply because their intention was just that—to be married, rather than to be fulfilled. And in the end, each of those couples had a relationship in which there was no regard for intimacy, growth, or building a strong life.

If you're feeling stuck in your life and want to move forward, start by examining your past motivations. Look closely—I've learned that my truest intentions are often hiding in the shadows. Ask yourself: *How have my intentions produced the experiences I'm having now? And if I change my intentions, what different consequences will I create?* As you make choices that honor who you are, you'll get exactly what life intended for you—the chance to reach your greatest potential.

I've *always had* a great relationship with money, even when I barely had any to relate to. I never feared not having it and never obsessed about what I had. Like most people, I can remember every salary I ever made. I suppose we remember because a salary helps define the value of our service—and, unfortunately for some people, the value they place on themselves.

I first realized I was not my salary when I was 15 and making 50 cents an hour babysitting Mrs. Ashberry's rowdy kids, and cleaning up after she pulled nearly every outfit from her closet every time she got dressed. Her bedroom always looked like the end-of-the-day, last-call sale at Macy's, with shoes and brightly colored necklaces and dresses everywhere. Just before flitting out the door (without leaving any info as to where she was going or how she could be reached), she'd say, "Oh, by the way, dear, would you mind tidying things up a bit?" Well, yes, of course I did mind, and the first time I "tidied up," I did such a great job, I thought surely she'd pay me extra when she saw how I cleaned not only her room but the kids' rooms, too. She never did. So I moved on and found a job that would pay me more—a job where I thought my efforts would be appreciated.

There was a five-and-dime not far from my father's store, and I got hired there for $1.50 an hour. My job was to keep things straight, stock shelves, fold socks. I wasn't allowed to work the cash register or speak to customers. I hated it. Two hours in, I found myself counting the minutes to lunch, then to quitting time. Even at 15 I knew in my soul this was no way to live, or make money. I was bored beyond anything I've ever felt before or since. So after three days, I quit and went to work in my father's store—for *no* salary. I didn't like working there, either, but at least I could talk to people and not feel like my spirit was being drained by the hour. Still, I knew that no matter how much my father wanted it to be, that store would not be a part of my future life.

By the time I was 17, I was working in radio, making $100 a week. And that's when I made my peace with money. I decided that no matter what job I ever did, I wanted that same feeling I got when I first started in radio—the feeling of *I love this so much, even if you didn't pay me I'd show up every day, on time and happy to be here.* I recognized then what I know now for sure: If you can get paid for doing what you love, every paycheck is a bonus. Give yourself the bonus of a lifetime: Pursue your passion. Discover what you love. Then do it!

I've *never been a* white-water-raftin', bungee-jumpin' kind of girl—that's not how I define adventure. What I know for sure is this: The most important adventure of our lives doesn't have to involve climbing the highest peak or trekking around the world. The biggest thrill you can ever achieve is to live the life of your dreams.

Maybe you're like so many women I've talked to over the years who have suspended their deepest desires in order to accommodate everything and everyone else. You ignore the nudge—that whisper that often comes in the form of emptiness or restlessness—to finally get on with what you know you should be doing. I understand how easy it is to rationalize: Your mate and your children need you; the job that you admit makes you miserable demands so much of your time. But what happens when you work hard at something unfulfilling? It drains your spirit. It robs you of your life force. You end up depleted, depressed, and angry.

You don't have to waste another day on that road. You can begin again. Starting over begins with looking inward. It means ridding yourself of distractions and paying attention to that inkling you've been ignoring. I've learned that the more stressful and chaotic things are on the outside, the calmer you need to get on the inside. It's the only way you can connect with where your spirit is leading you.

M*any years ago*, as a young television reporter at WJZ in Baltimore, I was given what was considered a plum assignment. I was sent to Los Angeles to interview a few television stars.

At first I was thrilled. Here was a chance to prove myself a good interviewer—alone, without the help of my usual co-anchor—and to add some celebrity cachet to my career experience. But by the time I arrived in California, I felt like a small fish dropped into the Hollywood fishbowl. I started to doubt myself: *Who was I to think I could just walk into their world and expect them to talk to me?* Reporters from all over the country had been invited. There were throngs of us local newscasters, entertainment/lifestyle reporters, each given five minutes to interview an actor from the TV season's upcoming lineup. I started to feel nervous. Uncomfortable. Inept. Not good enough to be there with all those other reporters from much bigger cities with more experience than I.

To make matters worse, a representative for Priscilla

Presley, who was there for a new show she was hosting, told me—as I was eleventh in line to talk to her—"You can ask her anything, but whatever you do, don't mention Elvis. She'll walk out on you." So now I wasn't just intimidated by this new world of "stars" and their handlers—I was feeling completely inhibited.

I'd been a TV reporter since I was 19. I'd interviewed hundreds of people in difficult situations and prided myself on being able to break the ice and establish rapport. But I wasn't accustomed to real "stars." I thought they had some mystique, that being famous made them not only different but also better than us regular folk. And I was having difficulty figuring out how I'd pull that off in a five-minute time frame with the most real questions being off-limits.

For some reason—you might call it a coincidence; I call it grace in action—I was switched from the Priscilla Presley line to interview a young comedian who was starting a new show called *Mork & Mindy*. What followed were five of the most exhilarating, wild, off-the-charts minutes I'd ever spent in an interview, with the most uninhibited, out-of-the-box, free-falling-in-every-second celebrity/human I'd ever met.

I don't remember a word I said (but I know I hardly said any). He was a geyser of energy. I remember thinking, *Whoever this guy is, he is going to be BIG.* He wasn't afraid to be his many selves. I had great fun playing with Robin Williams, and I learned in that instant to go where the interview takes you. He was all over the place, and I had to flow with it.

So when my turn came to talk to Miss Priscilla, I for sure had received the lesson: You can't accomplish anything worthwhile if you inhibit yourself.

I asked about Elvis. She didn't walk out. In fact, she obliged me with an answer.

If life teaches you nothing else, know this: When you get the chance, go for it.

M y *biggest mistakes* in life have all stemmed from giving my power to someone else—believing that the love others had to offer was more important than the love I had to give to myself. I remember being 29 and in a relationship based on lies and deceit, down on my knees crying after Mr. Man, once again, brought me low. I had been waiting for him all evening—he stood me up, arriving hours after our date, and I had dared to ask why. I remember him standing in the doorway and hurling these words at me: "The problem with you, baby doll, is that you think you're special." At which point he turned on his heels and slammed the door in my face.

I had grown up watching my cousin Alice be physically abused by her boyfriend, and I had vowed I would never take such treatment. But sitting there on the bathroom floor after he walked out, I saw with great clarity that the only difference between Alice and me was that I hadn't been hit. Mr. Man was wrong: I did *not* think I was special—and that was the problem. Why was I allowing myself to be treated this way?

Even with these insights it took me another year to end the relationship. I kept hoping and praying things would get better, that he would change. He never did. I started praying for the strength to end it. I'd pray and wait to feel better. And wait. And wait. All the while repeating my same old patterns.

Until one day I got it. While I was waiting on God, God was waiting on me. He was waiting on me to make a decision to either pursue the life that was meant for me or to be stifled by the one I was living. I recognized the truth that I am all right just as I am. I am enough all by myself.

That revelation brought its own miracle. Around that time the call came for me to audition for a talk show in Chicago. If I'd stayed entangled in that relationship, my life as I know it would never have happened.

What is the truth of your life? It's your duty to know.

In order to find out, know that the truth is that which feels right and good and loving. (Love doesn't hurt, I've learned in the years since I was 29. It feels really good.) It's that which allows you to live every day with integrity.

Everything you do and say shows the world who you are. Let it be the truth.

I'll *never forget* the moment when I decided to always choose myself. I recall what I was wearing (a blue turtleneck and black slacks), where I was sitting (in my boss's office), what the chair looked and felt like (brown paisley, too deep and overstuffed)—when my boss, the general manager at the Baltimore TV station where I worked, said, "There's no way you can make it in Chicago. You're walking into a land mine and you can't even see it. You're committing career suicide."

He used every tactic he could muster to entice me to stay—more money, a company car, a new apartment, and finally, intimidation: "You're going to fail."

I didn't know if he was right. I didn't have the confidence to believe I could succeed. But somehow I gathered the nerve to say to him before standing up and walking out, "You're right, I may not make it and I may be walking into land mines. But if they don't kill me, at least I'll keep growing."

In that moment, I chose happiness—the lasting happiness that abides with me every day because I decided not to be afraid and to move forward.

Staying in Baltimore would have been the safe thing to do. But sitting in my boss's office, I knew that if I let him talk me into staying, it would affect the way I felt about myself forever. I would always wonder what could have been. That one choice changed the trajectory of my life.

I live in a state of exhilarated contentment (my definition of happiness), fueled by a passion for everything I'm committed to: my work, my colleagues, my home, my gratitude for every breath taken in freedom and peace. And what makes it sweeter is knowing for sure that I created this happiness. It was my choice.

Time is fleeting. Those of you with children are ever cognizant of this fact—because your children keep growing out of and into themselves. The goal for all of us is to keep growing out of ourselves, too, evolving to our best possible lives.

Somewhere deep within me, even when I was a teenager, I always sensed that something bigger was in store for me—but it was never about attaining wealth or celebrity. It was about the process of continually seeking to be better, to challenge myself to pursue excellence on every level.

What I know for sure: Only when you make that process your goal can your dream life follow. That doesn't mean your process will lead you to wealth or fame—in fact, your dream may have nothing to do with tangible prosperity and everything to do with creating a life filled with joy, one with no regrets and a clear conscience. I've learned that, yes, wealth is a tool that gives you choices—but it can't compensate for a life not fully lived, and it certainly can't create a sense of peace within you. The whole point of being alive is to become the person you were intended to be, to grow out of and into yourself again and again.

I believe you can do this only when you stop long enough to hear the whisper you might have drowned out, that small voice compelling you toward your calling. And what happens then? You face the biggest challenge of all: to have the courage to seek your dream regardless of what anyone else says or thinks. You are the only person alive who can see your big picture—and even you can't see it all. The truth is that as much as you plan and dream and move forward in your life, you must remember you are always acting in conjunction with the flow and energy of the universe.

Move in the direction of your goal with all the force and verve you can muster—and then let go, releasing your plan to the Power that's bigger than yourself and allowing your dream to unfold as its own masterpiece. Dream big—very big. Work hard—very hard. And after you've done all you can, fully surrender to the Power.

Awe

———— ❧ ————

"In the word question, *there is a beautiful word—*
quest. I love that word."

—Elie Wiesel

I *no longer make* a list of New Year's resolutions. I do, however, give considerable thought every January as to how I can continue to move forward.

One New Year's morning, I was sitting on my front porch in Hawaii, overlooking the ocean, meditating. I prayed to be more resolved about being fully conscious, allowing every experience to bring me closer to the deepest essence of life.

By nightfall my prayer had been answered in the most profound spiritual encounter I've ever had.

My friend Bob Greene and I were taking a hike. The

sun had set, leaving wisps of lavender ribbons across the sky. Clouds moving down from the mountain spread out over the ocean, with only a small opening through which we could see the moon. All around us was the cloud mist and just one clear space of sky glowing with the light of a crescent moon.

"Look at that," Bob said. "It looks like the DreamWorks logo. I feel like climbing up and sitting there with a fishing pole."

It was surreal.

As we continued our walk, Bob turned to me and said, "Stop a minute."

I stopped.

"Can you hear that?" he whispered.

I could—and it took my breath away. "It" was the sound of silence. Utter and complete stillness. So still I could hear my own heart beating. I wanted to hold my breath, because even inhaling and exhaling was a cacophony. There was absolutely no movement, no breeze, no recognition of air, even; it was the sound of nothing and everything. It felt like all life . . . and death . . . and beyond contained in one space, and I was not just standing in it, I was also *part* of *it*. This was the most peaceful, coherent, knowledgeable moment I've ever experienced. Heaven on earth.

We stood there for the longest time. Trying not to breathe, in awe, I realized this was exactly what I had asked for earlier in the day. This is the meaning of "Ask, and it shall be given . . . seek, and ye shall find." That moment was indeed "the deepest essence of life." And what I know for sure: That moment is always available to us. If you peel back the layers of your life—the frenzy, the noise—stillness is waiting.

That stillness is you.

This is what I call a "glory, glory, hallelujah" moment. I wanted to hold on to it forever, and I have. Sometimes I'll be in the middle of a meeting, with people lined up outside my door, and I'll just inhale and take myself back to the road, the clouds, the moon. . . . Stillness. Peace.

I'm *often confronted by* things about which I have no certainty at all. But I for sure believe in miracles. For me, a miracle is seeing the world with light in your eyes. It's knowing there's always hope and possibility where none seems to exist. Many people are so closed to miracles that even when one is boldly staring them in the face, they label it coincidence. I call it like I see it. To me, miracles are confirmation that something larger than us is at work. I believe they happen not just sometimes but every single day, if we are open to seeing them.

In my own life, miracles often involve the simplest things, like being able to run five miles in less than fifty minutes. Or being exhausted after a long run and craving a bowl of red pepper and tomato soup—then walking into the kitchen to find that my godmother, Mrs. E, left some on the stove for me. A miracle is watching a sunset the color of strained peaches and seeing it turn to raspberries by the end of my evening walk. It's having pomegranate, kiwi, and mango on a pretty tray for breakfast. It's admiring the pink peonies I cut from my own garden and placed in my bedroom. It's when a green minivan pauses on the road and a young woman leans out the window to yell, "You're the best teacher on TV!"—and she herself is a kindergarten teacher. It's the sound of the birds and their individual songs and the moment when I wonder, *Are they singing to each other, to themselves, or just to be heard?*

A miracle is the chance to roll in the grass with all of my dogs—and enjoy a full Sunday stretched before me with no obligations, no plans, no place to be. It's the chance to come back to myself after a week of going, going, going and have time to finally just be—alone. To meditate on a log cabin porch, leaves rustling like water, newborn geese in the pond with their mother teaching them to swim. To feel the joy of this glorious life—and have the chance to live it as a free woman. If I know nothing else for sure, I know that the big miracles we're waiting on are happening right in front of us, at every moment, with every breath. Open your eyes and heart and you'll begin to see them.

G etting *older is* the best thing that ever happened to me.

I awaken to a morning prayer of thanks posted on my bathroom wall from Marianne Williamson's book *Illuminata*. Whatever age I'm at, I think about all the people who never made it that far. I think about the people who were called before they realized the beauty and majesty of life on earth.

I know for sure that every day holds within it the possibility of seeing the world with wonder.

The older I get, the less tolerance I have for pettiness and superficial pursuits. There's a wealth that has nothing to do with dollars, that comes from the perspective and wisdom of paying attention to your life. It has everything to teach you. And what I know for sure is that the joy of learning well is the greatest reward.

I 've heard *truly amazing* stories over the years, about almost every human situation. Conflict, defeat, triumph, resilience. But I've rarely been more awed than I was by John Diaz's story. In October 2000, John was on Singapore Airlines flight 006 when it exploded at takeoff. Eighty-three people perished in the flames. John and 95 others survived. John—who describes himself as a very straightforward, competitive, and pragmatic kind of guy—still endures physical pain from his injuries. But in other ways he is more alive than he was before he literally went through the fire.

The plane took off in typhoonlike conditions. Before John boarded, his instinct told him not to. He'd called the airline several times—"Are you sure this plane is taking off?"—because it was storming so badly. Peering out the window as the plane taxied, all he could see was rain. He was sitting in the very front of the plane and watched as the nose started to lift.

But the 747 had turned down the wrong runway.

At first he felt a small bump (the plane hitting a concrete barrier), followed by a huge bump right next to him where something (a backhoe) ripped a hole in the side of the plane right near where he was seated. His seat came unbolted and was thrown sideward. He could feel the motion of the plane rolling and spinning down the runway. And then it stopped. In his words:

"Then the explosion hit . . . a great fireball came right out and over me all the way up to the nose of the plane and then sucked straight back, almost like in the movies. And then there was this spray of jet fuel like napalm— whatever it hit . . . ignited like a torch. . . .

"And a gentleman, an Asian gentleman, comes running right up to me, fully aflame. I could see all his features, and there was a look of wonder on his face— like he didn't even know he was dead and burning. And I figured, well, I must be the same. I really thought at that point I was dead."

I asked John if he believed it was divine intervention that saved him. He said no. He said what helped him get out was his position in the plane and quick thinking: To protect himself from the smoke and flames, he covered his head with the leather bag he'd been encouraged not to carry on, then looked for the door and kept moving.

And then he shared something I still think about to this day.

The inside of the plane, John said, "looked like Dante's Inferno, with people strapped to their seats, just burning. It seemed like an aura was leaving their bodies—some brighter than others. . . . I thought the brightness and dimness of the auras were how one lives one's life." John says that experience—seeing what he could only describe as auras, an energy of light leaving the bodies and floating above the flames—changed him, made him a more empathetic person. And although he still won't call his brush with death a miracle, he does say, "I want to live my life so my aura, when it leaves, is very bright."

What I know for sure: It is an awesome gift to be alive on this beautiful planet. And I want my time here to be as bright as it can be.

I *know for sure* there is no real meaning to life without a spiritual component.

Spirit to me is the essence of who we are. It doesn't require any particular belief. It just is. And the key to this essence is simply being aware of the present moment. It's transformative. It redefines what it means to be alive.

Spirituality can be something as ordinary—and extraordinary—as giving your full-force, hundred-percent attention to another person, without thinking about what else you need to be doing right then. Or making an effort to do something good for someone. Or starting your day with a full moment of silence. Or waking up to literally smell the coffee, "tasting" its aroma through your senses, making every sip sheer pleasure, and when it's no longer sheer pleasure, putting it aside.

What I know for sure: The light in your life comes in, one conscious breath at a time.

Breathe easy.

M y *entire life is* a miracle. And so is yours. That I know for sure.

No matter how you came to be—whether you were wanted or "an accident" (as I was labeled for many years)—your being here to read these words is awesome.

I say this not knowing the details of your life. What I do know is that every person carries her own story of hope and sorrow, victory and loss, redemption, joy, and light.

Everyone has had her share of life lessons. How well you learn from them is up to you.

When you choose to see the world as a classroom, you understand that all experiences are here to teach you something about yourself. And that your life's journey is about becoming more of who you are. Another miracle: We all get to share in the journey.

The hardest experiences are often the ones that teach us the most. Whenever trouble comes my way I try to ask myself: "What is this really about, and what am I supposed to learn from it?" Only when I perceive what the real lesson is can I make the best decision—and grow from the experience.

After everything that's happened to me in all my years on this earth, what I'm most proud of is that I remain open to evolving. I know that every physical encounter has a metaphysical meaning. And I'm open to seeing it all.

I was *lucky enough* to spend some time in Fiji several years ago, and while I was there, I loved watching the waves break gently onshore.

I think of each ripple as each of us in the sea that is life. We believe we're all so different, but we're not. We cover ourselves in customs and costumes of aspiration, struggle and victory, sacrifice and loss—and soon forget who we really are.

One morning as I sat watching the waves, I e-mailed my poet friend Mark Nepo, whose *Book of Awakening* is a year's worth of daily lessons for living a more intentional life. Mark's e-mail response was this:

YOU ASK ABOUT POETRY

You ask from an island so far away
it remains unspoiled. To walk quietly
till the miracle in everything speaks

> is poetry. You want to look for poetry
> in your soul and in everyday life, as you
> search for stones on the beach. Four
> thousand miles away, as the sun ices
> the snow, I smile. For in this moment,
> you are the poem. After years of looking,
> I can only say that searching for
> small things worn by the deep is
> the art of poetry. But listening
> to what they say is the poem.

I never thought of poetry that way before. But sitting on the edge of an island, I could feel that what Mark said in the rest of his e-mail was also true:

"For me, poetry is the unexpected utterance of the soul. It is where the soul touches the everyday. It is less about words and more about awakening the sense of aliveness we carry within us from birth. To walk quietly till the miracle in everything speaks is poetry, whether we write it down or not. I confess I started out wanting to write great poems, only to be worn by life to wanting to discover true poems, and now in the second half of life, I feel humbled and excited to want to be the poem!"

That, for sure, is an aspiration worth holding: to not just appreciate the poetry, but to be the poem.

S pirituality for me is recognizing that I am connected to the energy of all creation, that I am a part of it—and it is always a part of me. Whatever label or word we use to describe "it" doesn't matter.

Words are completely inadequate. Spirituality is not religion. You can be spiritual and not have a religious context. The opposite is true, too: You can be very religious with no spiritual dimension, just doctrine.

Spirituality isn't something I believe in. It is what and who I am. Knowing this has made all the difference. It allows me to live fearlessly. And to make manifest the purpose of my creation. And I will be bold enough to say I know for sure it's the greatest discovery of life: to recognize that you're more than your body and your mind.

Over the years, I've read hundreds of books that have helped me become more spiritually attuned. One of them in particular, A New Earth, by Eckhart Tolle, resonated so deeply with me that it caused a shift in the way I perceived myself and all things. The book is essentially about recognizing that you are not your thoughts, and seeing, then changing, the way your ego-based mind dominates your life.

Allowing the truth of who you are—your spiritual self—to rule your life means you stop struggling and learn to move with the flow of your life. To quote from *A New Earth*: "There are three words that convey the secret of the art of living, the secret of all success and happiness: One With Life. Being one with life is being one with Now. You then realize that you don't live your life, but life lives you. Life is the dancer, and you are the dance."

The joy and vitality that come from being that dance are unmatched by any pleasure you can imagine. What it takes, I've learned, is being committed to experiencing life's spiritual essence. And that, as I've said in conversation with Eckhart Tolle, is a decision you make daily: to be in the world but not of it.

Remember the Internet rumors about the year 2012? For those of you not familiar with the prophecies of global change (based partly on the cycles of the Mayan calendar), suffice it to say that some people predicted a cataclysmic collapse of human civilization, while others foresaw a time of spiritual transformation.

Of course no one can predict the future, but one thing I do know for sure is the power of intention. And my intention is to approach every year as one of great promise. No doomsday for me: I hope to do my part, within myself and within the world, to bring about a shift that lets us live more authentically, more lovingly, more intuitively, more creatively, and more collaboratively. That's my idea of spiritual evolution. Of a spiritual revolution!

I chose to see 2012 as the dawning of a new year of alignment, because with alignment comes enlightenment. When you're aligned with your heart's desire, when you're in sync with who you're meant to be and how you're supposed to contribute to our magnificent earth, you feel a shift in perception. You start to notice moments of what some people call serendipity but I like to call marvelisms. Because when I'm doing everything I'm meant to do to keep my mind, body, and spirit whole, I constantly marvel at how other experiences fall into place. It's as though that beautiful line in Paulo Coelho's novel *The Alchemist* comes true: "When you want something, all the universe conspires in helping you to achieve it."

My goal: to stay open to all the universe has to offer. Every year. Every day.

O*ne of the things* I often ask God: Please show me who I really am.

That may seem like an odd question. But as I go through life, I want to never lose sight of the truth of my existence. One of my favorite life quotes comes from the French philosopher-priest Pierre Teilhard de Chardin: "We are not human beings having a spiritual experience. We are spiritual beings having a human experience."

To make that experience as purposeful and poetic as possible is my heart's single greatest desire for sure.

Breathe *with* *me* for a moment. Place your hands on your stomach and feel it expand as you inhale. Then let it contract and deflate as you exhale. That cycle happens, on average, 720 times an hour, more than 17,000 times a day—without your even thinking about it.

The biological wonder of a breath is so easy to take for granted, but every now and again I get still enough to notice it. And when I do: Wow! For sure I stand in awe of the miracle that is life.

Walking barefoot across an earthy carpet of freshly mown grass. Wow, it feels so good!

Another wow: Every night at sunset, friends and neighbors gather on my front porch to watch what we call the greatest show on Earth. We take pictures and compare the color variations of each magnificent light show as the sun dips below the horizon.

One day not long ago it rained for four hours straight. A steady downpour, and then suddenly it stopped. Wow! Everything—trees, fences, sky—was luminescent.

For me, nature is one great big wow after another, and sometimes its smallest offerings are the ones that open my soul to its splendor. For my birthday one year, a florist friend who has created spectacular arrangements of every sort gave me one of my most treasured gifts ever: two small leaves shaped like hearts. I keep them pressed between the pages of my favorite book, Eckhart Tolle's *A New Earth*. Every time I open it, I am reminded how simple and beautiful life can be—if we choose to see it that way.

*S*eeking *the fullest expression of self.* That's the story of my life in six words—my personal definition of what I'm all about, at least for now. I think of it as my mini-memoir, but in writing it I was reminded that my definition has always been and still is evolving. Words I would have used last year don't apply today. Because if we're really committed to growth, we never stop discovering new dimensions of self and self-expression.

A few years ago I went to Fairfield, Iowa—population 9,500, smack in the middle of Midwestern farmland, the last place you'd expect to get stuck in an evening traffic jam caused by hundreds of people heading off to practice transcendental meditation. But that's what they do in Fairfield; in fact, it's often referred to as TM Town. The action takes place in two golden dome-shaped buildings: one for the women, one for the men. Housewives, shop clerks, engineers, waitresses, lawyers, moms, single ladies, and me—we all gathered in our dome for the sole purpose of being still. Knowing that stillness is the space where all creative expression, peace, light, and love come to be.

It was a powerfully energizing yet calming experience. I didn't want it to end.

When it did, I walked away feeling fuller than when I'd come in. Full of hope, a sense of contentment, and profound joy. Knowing for sure that even in the daily craziness that bombards us from every direction, there is—still—the constancy of stillness.

Only from that space can you create your best work and your best life.

I try to give myself a healthy dose of quiet time at least once—and when I'm on point, twice—a day. Twenty minutes in the morning, twenty in the evening. It helps me sleep better and focus deeper; it boosts my productivity and fuels my creativity.

Try it yourself and I think you'll agree that Glinda the Good Witch was right: "You've always had the power." You just have to be still to find it. And when you do, you're on the way to finding the fullest expression of *you*.

I've *always thought of* myself as a seeker. And by that I mean my heart is open to seeing—in all forms—the divine order and exquisite perfection with which the universe operates.

I am beguiled by the mystery of life. As a matter of fact, on my nightstand I keep a book called *In Love with the Mystery*, by Ann Mortifee. It's full of tranquil photographs and bite-sized reminders of the preciousness of the wondrous journey we're all on.

Here is one of my favorite passages:

"Let the power come. Let ecstasy erupt. Allow your heart to expand and overflow with adoration for this magnificent creation and for the love, wisdom, and power that birthed it all. Rapture is needed now—rapture, reverence, and grace."

I find solace and inspiration in those words. Too often we block the power that is ever-present and available to us, because we're so wrapped up in *doing* that we lose sight of *being*.

I often wonder what Steve Jobs saw when he uttered his last words: "Oh, wow. Oh, wow. Oh, wow."

I wonder if it was the same vision the mother of a 26-year-old cancer patient shared on my show years ago. With his last breath, her son had said, "Oh, Mom, it's so simple."

I believe we make our paths far more difficult than they need to be. Our struggle with and resistance to *what is* entangles us in constant chaos and frustration—when it's all so simple. Do unto others as you would have them do unto you. And remember Newton's third law of motion: For every action there is an equal and opposite reaction. The energy you create and release into the world will be reciprocated on all levels.

Our main job in life is to align with the energy that is the source of all energies, and to keep our frequency tuned to the energy of love. This I know for sure.

When that is your life's work, mystery solved—or at least, the mystery no longer mystifies you. It only heightens the rapture, reverence, and grace.

As the day got closer, I couldn't stop silently rejoicing. I'd tell myself: *I'm turning 60!* I was so glad I'd lived long enough to say those words and celebrate their meaning.

I'm turning 60. I'm alive. Healthy. Strong.

I'm turning 60, and—please don't take offense—I no longer have to be concerned about what anyone thinks of me! (You know, the old "Am I doing it right?" "Am I saying it right?" "Am I being what or who I'm 'supposed' to be?")

When I turned 60, I knew for sure that I'd earned the right to be just as I am. I'm more secure in being myself than I've ever been.

I have reached the moment Derek Walcott describes in his beautiful poem "Love After Love"—" . . . with elation / you will greet yourself arriving/at your own door , in your own mirror/and each will smile at the other's welcome."

I am in awe of the way my journey here on earth continues to unfold. My life has been marked by miracles for as long as I can recall (and even before, considering that my entire existence is the result of a onetime frolic under an oak tree). My early days speaking in a Mississippi Methodist church—Baptist leanings, shoutin', and Holy Ghost included—prepared me for a future of speaking in a public arena I could never have imagined.

And now I simply want to share what I've been given. I want to continue to encourage as many people as I can to open their hearts to life, because if I know anything for sure, it's that opening my own heart is what has brought me my greatest success and joy.

My highest achievement: never shutting down my heart. Even in my darkest moments—through sexual abuse, a pregnancy at 14, lies and betrayals—I remained faithful, hopeful, and willing to see the best in people, regardless of whether they were showing me their worst. I continued to believe that no matter how hard the climb, there is always a way to let in a sliver of light to illuminate the path forward.

We go through life discovering the truth about who we are and determining who has earned the right to share the space within our heart.

This I also know for sure: God—however you define

or refer to Him, Her, or It—is for us. The forces of nature are for us, offering us life in abundance. We humans narrow what is an open field of wonder and majesty to the myopic reality of our day-to-day experiences. But there is extraordinary in the ordinary.

Some days the awareness of the sanctity and sacredness of life brings me to my knees with gratitude. I'm still trying to wrap my head around the idea that the little girl from Mississippi who grew up holding her nose in an outhouse now flies on her own plane—my own plane!—to Africa to help girls who grew up like her. *Amazing grace, how sweet the sound!*

I approached the milestone of 60 with humility, supreme thanksgiving, and joy. Knowing for sure *grace has brought me safe thus far, and grace will lead me home.*

Clarity

———— ❧ ————

"First say to yourself what you would be;
and then do what you have to do."

—Epictetus

I *was 40 years old* before I learned to say no. In my early
years of working in television, I was often overwhelmed
by people's view of me as a benevolent caregiver. Some
would spend their last dime on a bus ticket to get to me,
children would run away from home, abused women would
leave their husbands and show up at the doorstep of my
studio, all hoping I'd help. In those days, I'd spend a lot
of energy trying to get a girl back to her family or hanging
on the phone with someone who was threatening to kill
herself. I found myself writing check after check, and over
time that wore on my spirit. I was so busy trying to give all

that everyone else needed me to offer that I lost touch with what I had a genuine desire to give. I'd been consumed by the disease to please—and often the word yes would be out of my mouth before I even knew it.

I know exactly where the disease came from. Having a history of abuse also meant a history of not being able to set boundaries. Once your personal boundaries have been violated as a child, it's difficult to regain the courage to stop people from stepping on you. You fear being rejected for who you really are. So for years, I spent my life giving everything I could to almost anyone who asked. I was running myself ragged trying to fulfill other people's expectations of what I should do and who I should be.

What cured me was understanding the principle of intention. To quote Gary Zukav again, from his book *The Seat of the Soul*, "Every action, thought and feeling is motivated by an intention, and that intention is a cause that exists as one with an effect. If we participate in the cause, it is not possible for us not to participate in the effect. In this most profound way, we are held responsible for our every action, thought and feeling, which is to say, for our every intention."

I started to examine the intention behind my saying yes when I really meant no. I was saying yes so people wouldn't be angry with me, so they would think I was a nice person. My intention was to make people feel I was the one they could call on, count on, last minute, no matter what. And that was exactly what my experiences reflected—a barrage of requests in every aspect of my life.

Shortly after I started to understand this, I got a call from somebody quite famous who wanted me to donate to his charity. He was asking for a lot of money, and I told him I had to think about it. What I thought about was, *Is this a cause I really believe in?* No. *Do I really think that writing a check is going to make any difference whatsoever?* No. So why would I do it? *Because I don't want this person to think I'm stingy.* This was no longer a good enough reason for me.

I wrote down a few words, which I now keep on my desk: "Never again will I do anything for anyone that I do not feel directly from my heart. I will not attend a meeting, make a phone call, write a letter, sponsor or participate in any activity in which every fiber of my being does not resound yes. I will act with the intent to be true to myself."

Before you say yes to anyone, ask yourself: What is my truest intention? It should come from the purest part of you, not from your head. If you have to ask for advice, give yourself time to let a yes or no resound within you. When it's right, your whole body feels it.

I know for sure that I had to first get clear about who I was before I could beat the disease to please. When I accepted that I was a decent, kind, and giving person—whether I said yes or no—I no longer had anything to prove. I was once afraid of people saying, "Who does she think she is?" Now I have the courage to stand and say, "*This* is who I am."

I'm not nearly *as stressed* as people might imagine. Over the years, I've learned to focus my energy on the present, to be fully aware of what's happening in every moment and not to worry about what should have happened, what's going wrong, or what might come next. Yet because I do have an awful lot on my plate, if I didn't find a way to decompress, I'd be totally ineffective—and probably a little crazy, too.

None of us is built to run nonstop. That's why, when you don't give yourself the time and care you need, your body rebels in the form of sickness and exhaustion. How do I give back to myself? Hardly a day goes by that I don't talk things out with Gayle. Almost every night, I soak in a hot bath and light a candle or two. It may sound hokey, but focusing on a burning candle for a minute while taking deep and relaxing breaths is very calming. In the evenings right before sleep, I don't read or watch anything— including late-night news—that would give me anxiety. And because I don't like fitful dreams, I protect my sleep by dealing with difficult situations during my waking hours. I also keep a gratitude journal and, at the end of a workday, I "come down" by reading a great novel or just sitting with myself to come back to my center—it's what I call "going mindless."

As women we've been programmed to sacrifice everything in the name of what is good and right for everyone else. Then if there's an inch left over, maybe we can have a piece of that. We need to deprogram ourselves. I know for sure that you can't give what you don't have. If you allow yourself to be depleted to the point where your emotional and spiritual tank is empty and you're running on fumes of habit, everybody loses. Especially you.

I once taped a show in which a life coach discussed the concept of self-care—putting your own needs ahead of anyone else's—and the audience booed. Women were upset by the mere suggestion that they should put their needs before those of their children. I interrupted to explain: No one was saying you should abandon your children and let them starve. The life coach was suggesting that you nurture yourself so you'll have more nurturing to give to those who most need you. It's the airplane oxygen-mask theory: If you don't put on your mask first, you won't be able to save anyone else.

So stop and take a look at your own needs. Go mindless. Let go. And remind yourself that this very moment is the only one you know you have for sure.

*W*hat I know for sure is that your breath is your anchor, the gift you've been given—that we've all been given, to center ourselves in this very moment. Whenever I have an encounter that involves even the slightest tension, I stop, draw in a deep breath, and release. Ever notice how often you unconsciously hold your breath? Once you start paying attention, it might surprise you to see how much tension you've been carrying around inside. Nothing is more effective than a deep, slow inhale and release for surrendering what you can't control and focusing again on what's right in front of you.

Here's a confession: I have a fear of flying over the ocean. Though anytime I get on a plane it's a flight of faith, a belief in something greater than myself— aeronautics, God—flying over the ocean is particularly disconcerting. (I'm not that good a swimmer.) But when I have to cross continents, I just do it, because I want to be bigger than my fear.

I bought a home on a Hawaiian mountain because it was what I imagined paradise to be, knowing that every time I had to cross the Pacific to get there, I would challenge my fear.

The day after Christmas a few years ago, my plane had been airborne long enough for us to pull out Scrabble and start thinking about lunch. Urania, my friend Bob Greene's wife, had brought leftovers from Christmas dinner.

"No more mashed potatoes for me," I said. "I'll just have turkey—dark meat, preferably—and green beans."

Our flight attendant, Karin, leaned over the table. I thought she was going to say, "There's no dark meat left," but instead she said calmly, "There's a slight crack in the windshield; we're going to have to turn around."

"Oh," I replied.

"The captain wants you to strap yourselves in and be ready for oxygen masks."

"Oxygen masks? What will happen to my dogs?" They were lounging nearby.

"They'll be fine," Karin said. "We're going to drop to ten thousand feet now."

I could feel my heart pounding and my voice rising, though I was trying to mirror her calmness. My mind was speeding: *Oxygen! Danger! Oxygen! Danger! I can't swimmmmm. Oh, my dear God!!!!*

I didn't speak, but Karin later said my eyes were as big as plums. Stedman, steady as a boulder, took my hand, looked me in the eye, and said, "You're going to be fine. God didn't bring you this far to leave you. Remember that."

The crack had spread and shattered the entire left side of the windshield. We could see it from our seats. *Whoosh, thump, whoosh, thump.* I know all the familiar sounds on that aircraft, and this was something different. I don't like hearing something different at 40,000 feet.

"What's that noise, Karin?"

"We're depressurizing the cabin, lowering altitude quickly, and that sound is the oxygen pump. The pilots are on oxygen, just in case."

I didn't ask, "Just in case *what?*" because we all knew the answer. Just in case that windshield blew.

The pilots, Terry and Danny, turned the plane around, and I watched the clock: 27 minutes to landing. I thought, What if I'd listened to my inner voice and not flown today? Several times that morning I had wanted to cancel. I was feeling off balance, rushed. I'd called Bob Greene and said, "I may not go today."

"Why?" he said.

"Not feeling it. What do you think?"

"I think you should consult that trusted inner voice of yours."

I had taken a bath, since the tub is where I do my best thinking, and got out ready to call the pilots and postpone the trip. And then I didn't. I overrode that feeling. If I hadn't, would the windshield still have cracked? No doubt. But would we have been over the ocean with no place to land?

I looked at the clock again: 26 minutes and 12 seconds until landing.

I was going to lose my mind watching that clock, so I started to read. Soon, I felt a resolved calm. We'll be all right, no matter the outcome. The *whoosh, thump* became a source of comfort: Oxygen! Life! Oxygen! Life!

We landed safely, of course. The windshield was replaced, and the day after, the pilots said, "We can fly anytime you're ready." Did I dare fly over the ocean again so soon? What was the lesson for me? Did I get it?

I know for sure that whenever your inner GPS is off-kilter, trouble awaits. Your instincts are your compass. I got it. I get it. I know it for sure. Up in the air I relearned the importance of tuning out distraction and tuning in to myself.

O*ne of the most* important questions a woman can ask herself: What do I really want—and what is my spirit telling me is the best way to proceed?

My answer eventually led me toward my passion for serving women and girls. I have a deep understanding of what it's like to be a girl who has suffered abuse or lived in poverty, and I believe that education is the door to freedom, the rainbow that leads to the pot of gold. I began to realize that in order to be most effective, I had to be extremely focused on using my time, my concern, my resources, and my compassion to uplift a generation of courageous women who own themselves and know their strength. I knew I couldn't save every dying child or intervene in every case of abuse. None of us can. But once I got clear about what I most wanted to give, much of what didn't line up with that intention naturally fell away.

Those years of becoming focused taught me a powerful lesson about letting go of the outside pressures and distractions and instead tuning in to my gut—that inkling that says, *Hold on. Something's not right here. Please pause and make an adjustment.* For me, *doubt* often means *don't*. Don't move. Don't answer. Don't rush forward. When I'm mired in uncertainty about what the next step should be, when I'm asked to do something for which I feel little enthusiasm, that's my sign to just stop—to get still until my instincts give me the go-ahead. I believe that uncertainty is my spirit's way of whispering, *I'm in flux. I can't decide for you. Something is off balance here.* I take that as a cue to re-center myself before making a decision. When the universe compels me toward the best path to take, it never leaves me with "Maybe," "Should I?" or even "Perhaps." I always know for sure when it's telling me to proceed— because everything inside me rises up to reverberate "Yes!"

*A*round my fiftieth birthday, I became more aware of time than I had ever been. I felt an almost primal understanding in the core of myself that there was a finite amount of time left, and that feeling permeated everything I did, dictating how I reacted in every moment. It made me more conscious and appreciative of every experience, every awakening (*Gee, I'm still here; I have another chance today to get it right*). I still try to take in all experiences, even the negative ones. I take the time, even if it's only one minute in the morning, to breathe slowly and let myself feel the connection to all other breathing and vibrating energies in this world and beyond. I have found that recognizing your relationship to infinity makes the finite more palatable.

What I know for sure is that giving yourself time to just be is essential to fulfilling your mission as a human being. So I give myself Sundays. Sometimes I spend the whole day in my pajamas, sometimes I have church under the trees communing with nature. Most times I just do nothing—piddling, I call it—and let my brain and body decompress. Whenever I've slipped up and missed a Sunday, I've noticed a definite change in my disposition for the rest of the week. I know for sure that you cannot give to everybody else and not give back to yourself. You will end up empty, or at best, less than what you can be for yourself and your family and your work. Replenish the well of yourself, for yourself. And if you think there's no time to do that, what you're really saying is, "I have no life to give to or live for myself." And if you have no life to live for yourself, then why are you here?

About a decade ago I learned a big lesson. The phone was always ringing on Sundays, when I had set that aside as my time. I'd answer and feel agitated and irritable with the person who'd called. Stedman said to me on one of those occasions, "If you don't want to talk, why do you keep picking up the phone?" Aha moment: Just because the phone is ringing doesn't mean I have to respond. I control what I do with my time. We all do, even when it seems out of control. Protect your time. It is your life.

M any times we insist on having all the best things because that's the only way we can ensure "quality of life" for ourselves. I can neglect myself in every other way, but if I have the best watch or pocketbook or car or square footage, I get to tell myself I'm the best and how much I deserve to have even more of the best.

What I know for sure: Having the best *things* is no substitute for having the best *life*. When you can let go of the desire to acquire, you know you are really on your way.

I never *thought I'd hear* myself say this, but I've grown to enjoy lifting weights. I relish the sense of strength and discipline that comes when the muscles are forced to resist. Better still, lifting weights has taught me something about life.

I've tried varying schedules—lifting every day, every other day, two days on and a day off. The everyday approach was the least effective; constant lifting begins to break down the muscle tissue. The same is true with mind and spirit. Without giving yourself a chance to reenergize, you begin to break down all the connective fibers of your life.

Keeping it all straight is stressful. You need to give yourself moments to rest. I once told my assistant just because I have ten free minutes on my calendar doesn't mean I want to fill them. "Let's practice what my philosophy preaches," I said. That meant breathing space had to become part of my daily routine.

So I began scheduling little moments of calm—moments in which I do nothing for at least ten minutes. Sometimes I just rub my dog's belly, or play a little fetch. Or I take a stroll, or just sit still at my desk. It works wonders. Whenever I give myself these little breaks, I find I have more energy, and I'm in a better mood for all the business that comes afterward.

I know for sure that a little restoration goes a long way. I don't carry even a twinge of guilt about giving myself that time. I'm refilling my tank so that when the next phase begins, I'll be fired up and ready for whatever is to come. Fully restored.

I always thought I knew why exercise was essential—to not have a fat tush—but I didn't get the *real* reason until a visit to Johannesburg in 2005. I was visiting the Leadership Academy for Girls, the school I was building at the time, and knew there were many things on my agenda. I was jet-lagged when I arrived, so at 7 o'clock the next morning, I chose not to get up and work out. Instead, I stayed in bed an extra hour to catch up on rest. That was my excuse the first day. By the third day, it was about the treadmill. I didn't like it—not enough cushion support for my knees. After three days of not exercising, my resolve to stay fit dissipates. It's easier to lie to myself: *I'm too tired, too busy, there's not enough time* are all part of the downward spiral.

Unfortunately for me, the resolve to work out is directly tied to the resolve to eat healthfully—if one slips, so does the other.

The food at the hotel was not to my liking, so I made a special request for something anyone can make: mashed potatoes. The chefs had no problem whipping some up. And so I ate mashed potatoes and bread every night for the duration of my stay, which was ten days. Ten days of high-glycemic foods combined with no working out equals ten extra pounds for me.

Even worse than the weight gain was the way I felt. Exhausted. Lethargic. I suddenly had aches and strains I didn't know existed.

Aha! I finally got it: When you nurture and support your body, it reciprocates. The basis of that support is exercise, like it or not. The most essential benefit is more energy; weight control is a bonus. I know for sure that taking care of your body, no matter what, is an investment, and the return is priceless.

Among the many things I learned from Eckhart Tolle's A New Earth was this: I am not my body. After studying Tolle's ideas closely, I felt far more connected to consciousness, or soul, or inner spirit—whatever you choose to name the formless being that is the essence of who we are. I thought of all the years I'd wasted, hating myself fat and wanting myself thin; feeling guilty about every croissant, then giving up carbs, then fasting, then dieting, then worrying when I *wasn't* dieting, then eating everything I wanted until the next diet (on Monday or after the holidays or the next big event). All that wasted time, abhorring the thought of trying on clothes, wondering what was going to fit, what number the scale would say. All that energy I could have spent loving what is.

Who I am, who you are . . . I know for sure we're not our bodies or the image we hold of them. But because what you give your attention to looms larger—in this case, literally—all my focus on weight actually made me fatter. I can look at a picture from any period of my life, and the first thing that comes to mind is not the event or experience, but my weight and size, because that is how I've viewed (and judged) myself—through the prism of numbers. Such wasted time.

I've given up scale-watching—no longer will I let a number determine how I see myself and whether I'm worthy of a good day. It was an awakening to recognize how shallow and small that made me. You're not your body, and for sure you're not your body image.

I *try not to waste time*—because I don't want to waste myself. I'm working on not letting people with dark energy consume any of my minutes on this earth. I've learned that the hard way, after giving up hours of myself and my time, which are synonymous when you think about it. I've learned from my experiences of getting sucked into other people's ego dysfunction that their darkness robs you of your own light—the light you need to be for yourself and for others. What I know for sure is that how you spend your time defines who you are. And I want to shine my light for good.

Yes, I freely admit it: I have too many shoes. I also have too many jeans, and a designer bonanza of black skirts, size 8 to elastic. Plus tank tops and T-shirts and sweaters. In other words, I have issues with having too much stuff. I'm starting to ask myself this question: Do my things promote joy, beauty, and usefulness, or are they just burdensome?

I've decided to keep only that which delights me or enhances my well-being. Organizational expert Peter Walsh says in his book *Enough Already!* that our homes are "overwhelmed with stuff and [our] lives littered with the empty promises that the stuff didn't fulfill. . . . In buying what we want, we hope to acquire the life we desire. . . . [But] chasing the life you want by accumulating more stuff is a dead-end street."

This I know: More things don't make you feel more alive. Yet feeling more alive is part of fulfilling your true self. It's the reason we're all here.

Material excess is about so much more than the physical objects themselves. Although we know we need to let things go, doing so causes anxiety. Yet I know that letting go leaves space for more to come. That's true of our relationship not just to shoes but to all things. Cleaning house—both literally and metaphorically—is a great way to hit the Refresh button.

There are all kinds of ways to declutter your life—and they have nothing to do with just donating shoes.

Say good riddance to decisions that don't support self-care, self-value, and self-worth.

Ask yourself if the people in your life give you energy and encourage your personal growth, or block that growth with dysfunctional dynamics and outdated scripts. If they don't support you as a loving, open, free, and spontaneous being, good-bye!

Put a stop to the stagnant patterns that no longer serve you.

At work, reduce not only the "clutter" of inefficiency, but also strive to create a balanced workload and make your work invigorating, inspiring, collaborative, and empowering to others.

I want to be lean and clean for the future, dust off my wings. I know for sure that doing so will make it easier to fly. Enough already with the stuff that doesn't enhance who we really are. That's the real deal of decluttering, a process that's ever evolving as you move closer to the self you were meant to be.

And saying good-bye to too many shoes is a darn good start.

Power

———— ❦ ————

"When you know better, you do better."

—Maya Angelou

Whenever *I hear* Paul Simon's song "Born at the Right Time," I think he must be singing about me. I came into the world in 1954 in Mississippi—a state with more lynchings than any other in the Union—at a time when being a black man walking down the street minding your business could make you subject to any white person's accusation or whimsy. A time when having a good job meant working for a "nice" white family that at least didn't call you nigger to your face. A time when Jim Crow reigned, segregation prevailed, and black teachers, themselves scarcely educated, were forced to use ragged textbooks discarded from white schools.

Yet the same year I was born, a season of change began. In 1954 the Supreme Court ruled in *Brown vs. Board of Education* that black people had the right to equal education. The ruling created hope that life could be better for black folks everywhere.

I have always believed free will is a birthright, part of the universe's design for us. And I know that every soul yearns to be free. In 1997, while I was preparing to play Sethe in the movie *Beloved*, I arranged a trip along a portion of the Underground Railroad. I wanted to connect with what it felt like to be a slave wandering through the woods, making my way north to a life beyond slavery—a life where being free, at its most basic level, meant not having a master telling you what to do. But when I was blindfolded, taken into the woods, and left alone to contemplate which direction led to the next "safe house," I understood for the first time that freedom isn't about not having a master. Freedom is about having a choice.

In the film, Sethe explains what it was like to make the trek to freedom: "Looked like I loved [my children] more after we got here," she says. "Or maybe I knew as long as we were in Kentucky . . . they really weren't mine to love. . . . Sometimes I hear my boys, hear 'em laughing a laugh I ain't never heard. First I get scared, scared somebody might hear 'em and get mad. Then I remember that if they laugh that hard till it hurt, that be the only hurt they have all day." She also says, "I'd wake up in the mornin' and decide for myself what to do with the day," as if thinking: *Imagine, me decide*.

During shooting, I said those lines over and over, feeling the force they carried. In the years since, Sethe's words have remained with me—I rejoice in them daily. Sometimes they're my very first thought before I get out of bed. I can wake up in the morning and decide for myself what to do with the day—*Imagine, me decide*. What a gift that is.

What I know for sure is that we all need to cherish that gift—to revel in it rather than take it for granted. After the hundreds of stories I've heard of atrocities around the globe, I know that if you're a woman born in the United States, you're one of the luckiest women in the world. Take your good fortune and lift your life to its highest calling. Understand that the right to choose your own path is a sacred privilege. Use it. Dwell in possibility.

I've *always been* a homebody. I know that might be hard to believe, given my full schedule, but I usually head home right after work, finish dinner before 7:00, and climb into bed by 9:30. Even on weekends, home is my all-time favorite hangout. Since I've spent most of my adult life in the public eye, it's important for me to carve out a private space. A refuge. A safe house.

Years ago, Goldie Hawn told me she'd created her own safe haven by declaring her home a gossip-free zone. As part of her work for Words Can Heal, a national campaign to eliminate verbal violence, she and her family pledged to replace words that belittle and do damage with those that encourage and rebuild. Her choice to use language that uplifts is in line with a truth Maya Angelou once passed on to me: "I'm convinced that the negative has power—and if you allow it to perch in your house, in your mind, in your life, it can take you over," she said. "Those negative words climb into the woodwork, into the furniture, and the next thing you know, they're on your skin. A negative statement is poison."

I know firsthand just how hurtful negative words can be. Early in my career, when the tabloids began printing untruthful things about me, I was devastated. I felt so misunderstood. And I wasted a lot of energy worrying about whether people would believe the falsehoods. I had to fight the urge to get on the phone with anyone who'd maligned me and defend myself.

That was before I understood what I now know for sure: When someone spreads lies about you, it's not about you. Ever. Gossip—whether in the form of a rumor that's sweeping the nation or a gripe session between friends— reflects the insecurity of those who initiate it. Often when we make negative statements about others behind their backs, it's because we want to feel powerful—and that's usually because in some way we feel powerless, unworthy, not courageous enough to be forthright.

Hurtful words send the message—both to ourselves and to those with whom we share them—that we can't be trusted. If someone is willing to tear down one "friend," why wouldn't she be willing to disparage another? Gossip means we haven't emboldened ourselves to talk directly to the people we take issue with, so we belittle them. Playwright Jules Feiffer calls it committing little murders: Gossip is an assassination attempt by a coward.

We live in a culture obsessed with gossip—who's wearing what, who's dating whom, who's entangled in the latest sex scandal. What would happen if we declared our homes, our relationships, our lives a gossip-free zone? We'd probably be surprised at how much time we'd free up to do the work that's most significant—building our dreams rather than tearing down others'. We'd fill our homes with a spirit of truth that makes visitors want to kick off their shoes and stay awhile. And we'd remember that while words have the power to destroy, they also have the power to heal.

Some people might find it ironic that I've never been much of a TV watcher. Aside from old reruns of *The Andy Griffith Show*, I stopped regularly tuning in to sitcoms the night Mary Tyler Moore went off the air. At home, I skip the late-night news because I don't want to take in all that negative energy right before sleep—and on vacation, I seldom have a TV in my bedroom. On days when I do flip through the channels, it's almost certain I'll find at least one show that involves sexual exploitation or violence against women.

In my early days on-air, I was guilty of doing irresponsible television without even knowing it—all in the name of "entertainment." One day my staff and I booked a husband who'd been caught in an adulterous sex scandal, and right there on our stage before millions of viewers, the wife heard for the first time that her partner had been unfaithful. It's a moment I have never forgotten: The humiliation and despair on that woman's face made me ashamed of myself for putting her in that position. Right then I decided I'd never again be part of a show that demeans, embarrasses, or diminishes another human being.

I know for sure that what we dwell on is who we become—as a woman thinks, so she is. If we absorb hour upon hour of images and messages that don't reflect our magnificence, it's no wonder we walk around feeling drained of our life force. If we tune in to dozens of acts of brutality every week, it shouldn't surprise us that our children see violence as an acceptable way to resolve conflict.

Become the change you want to see—those are words I live by. Instead of belittling, uplift. Instead of demolishing, rebuild. Instead of misleading, light the way so that all of us can stand on higher ground.

There I am, sitting in Mr. Hooper's fifth-period algebra class, dreading the test we're about to take, when an announcement over the intercom tells us to go to the auditorium for a special guest speaker. *Hooray, I've been saved!* I say to myself, figuring that'll be the end of algebra for today.

My escape is the only thing on my mind as my classmates and I enter the room, single file. I settle into my seat and prepare to be bored to sleep in yet another assembly. But when the speaker is introduced as the Reverend Jesse Jackson, a civil rights leader who was with Dr. King the day he was shot, I sit up a little straighter. What I don't yet know is that I'm about to hear the speech of a lifetime.

It was 1969. Because I was an A to B student, I thought I already understood the importance of doing my best. But that day, Reverend Jackson lit a fire in me that changed the way I see life. His speech was about the personal sacrifices that had been made for all of us, regardless of how our ancestors came to be here. He talked about those who'd gone before us, who'd paved the way for us to be sitting in an integrated high school in Nashville. He told us that what we owed ourselves was excellence.

"Excellence is the best deterrent to racism," he said. "Therefore, be excellent."

I took him at his word. That evening I went home, found some construction paper, and made a poster bearing his challenge. I taped that poster to my mirror, where it stayed through my college years. Over time I added my own maxims: "If you want to be successful, be excellent." "If you want the best the world has to offer, offer the world your best."

Those words have helped me over many a hurdle, even when less than my best was evident. To this day, excellence is my intention. To be excellent in giving. In graciousness. In effort. In struggle and in strife. For me, being excellent means always doing my personal best. In Don Miguel Ruiz's book *The Four Agreements*, the final agreement is just that: Always do your best. I know for sure that this is the most fulfilling path to personal freedom. Your best varies from day to day, Ruiz says, depending on how you're feeling. No matter. Give your best in every circumstance so that you have no reason to judge yourself and create guilt and shame. Live so that at the end of each day, you can say, "I did my very best." That's what it means to excel at the great work of living your best life.

My *father raised me* to believe that being in debt was a terrible thing. In our house, it was almost a character flaw, akin to laziness and what he called "trifling." So when I moved away from home and was $1,800 in debt within a year, I felt I'd failed. I never told my father, nor would I have dared to borrow money from him.

Instead, I took out a consolidation loan at 21 percent interest, ate a lot of raisin bran for dinner, and bought the cheapest car I could afford—a bucket on wheels, I used to call it, but it got me to and from work. I tithed 10 percent to the church and shopped for clothes only once a year.

I paid off the $1,800 and vowed never again to create more bills than I could pay. I just hated the way overspending made me feel.

My dad saved for everything that mattered—a washer and dryer, a new refrigerator. By the time I left home in Nashville in 1976, he still hadn't gotten a new TV. He said his "money wasn't right." When *The Oprah Winfrey Show* went national, that's the first thing I bought him—a color TV, paid for in cash.

Why anyone chooses to live a life in debt has always been a puzzle to me. I'll never forget a couple who appeared on my show to talk about their financial plight. They'd been married for only nine months, but their relationship was already buckling beneath the weight of a gigantic expense. They'd charged most of their beach wedding in Mexico, paying for hotel rooms and spa treatments for some of their guests, lobster and filet mignon for the wedding dinner, and an open bar. On the other side of this blessed event were credit card bills for almost $50,000. That didn't include the $9,000 the husband had borrowed from his 401(k) plan to buy the engagement ring. The pursuit of a fairy-tale weekend had landed them in a nightmare that lasted for years.

What I know for sure: When you define yourself by the things you can acquire rather than see what you really need to be happy and fulfilled, you're not just living beyond your means or overextending yourself. You're living a lie.

That's why being burdened with bills feels so awful.

You are being untrue to yourself. When you free yourself from debt, you create space to purchase with purpose—to add to your life things that are meaningful.

I still think twice before I buy anything. How will this fit in with what I already have? Am I just caught up in the moment? Can it be of real use to me or is it just something beautiful to have? I still remember the time, years ago, when I was in an antiques store and the dealer showed me a gorgeous eighteenth-century dressing table with mirrors and hidden drawers. It was polished to such a sheen that the cherrywood seemed to be vibrating. But as I stood pondering whether to purchase it, I said to the man, "You're right—it's beautiful and I've never seen one quite like it—but I don't really need a dressing table with all that razzle-dazzle." He took a pretentious breath and replied, "Madam, no one buys anything here because of their needs—these are treasures to be enjoyed." Indeed. *Well, let me get down to the "needs" store*, I thought, *because what I'm really looking for are fireplace utensils*. Not only did I not need a dressing table, I hadn't the space for it.

To be fair, Mr. Dealer had a point—some things are just to be treasured and enjoyed.

But I know for sure that you enjoy everything a lot more when you're not overreaching. This is how you know you've shopped smart: You bring home a purchase, there's not a tinge of remorse, and whatever you got feels better to you ten days later than it did when you first bought it.

In 1988 I was in Tiffany's trying to decide between two china patterns. I was going back and forth, and finally my shopping buddy said, "Why don't you get both? You can afford to." I still remember thinking, *Oh my God. . . . I can. I can. I can get both!* I started jumping up and down right there in the store like I'd won the lottery.

Since that time, I've had many shopping temptations. But knowing that mindfulness matters in all experiences, I try to remain grounded. Another yellow sweater is going to make me feel . . . what? If the answer is "nothing," I'll put it back or get it for someone whose day it will brighten (like Gayle, who loves yellow the way some people love chocolate).

I hope the way you spend your money is in line with the truth of who you are and what you care about. I hope that your money brings joy to you and the ones you love. And I hope you use it as a powerful force for good to fulfill your best intentions.

I n my *twenties*, I attended a prayer breakfast in Washington, D.C., that was sponsored by the National Black Caucus. I had the good fortune to hear a most eloquent preacher from Cleveland: Reverend Otis Moss Jr., a man who would go on to become a mentor and friend.

That day, Reverend Moss told a story that abides with me to this day. His father, a poor sharecropper, worked all his life to raise and care for his family, suffering the same sort of indignities and humiliations that generations before him had long endured. But in his fifties, he finally had a chance to do what those generations never had: cast his vote in an election. On election day, he rose before dawn, dressed in his best suit, the one he wore to weddings and funerals, and prepared to walk to the polls to vote against a racist Georgia governor in favor of a moderate. Six miles he walked; when he got there, he was told he was in the wrong place and was sent to another location. He walked another five or six miles and was met with the same denial before being sent to a third voting place. When he arrived at the third location, they told him, "Boy, you are a little late—the polls just closed." After walking all day, covering more than 18 miles, he returned home, exhausted and depleted, never having experienced the joy of voting.

Otis Moss Sr. told this story to anyone who would listen, and lived in great anticipation of his next chance to cast his vote. He died before the next election. He never got that chance to choose. So now I do. And every time I cast a ballot, I choose not only for myself but also for Otis Moss Sr. and for the countless others who wanted to but couldn't. I cast a ballot for everybody who came before me and gave their life's energy so that yours and mine could be a force that matters today.

Sojourner Truth, speaking at the Women's Rights Convention in Akron in 1851, said, "If the first woman God ever made was strong enough to turn the world upside down all alone, these women together ought to be able to turn it back, and get it right side up again!" We'd see amazing changes if women took to the polls en masse.

Recent voting statistics are embarrassing and disrespectful to our female heritage—to every woman who had no voice but hoped someday her daughters might be heard. In 2008, only about two-thirds of eligible female voters bothered to cast a ballot. And remember, the 2000 presidential election was decided by only 537 votes. I know for sure: We ought to respect ourselves and our forebears enough to be counted.

W e're a *country that* spends 95 percent of our health care dollars on treating illness, and less than 5 percent on staying well and preventing it. How mixed up is that? The paradigm needs to change. And the change begins with how we choose to see ourselves: as purveyors of health or as conveyors of disease.

The ultimate in being healthy is to operate at full throttle—physically, emotionally, and spiritually. It's being alert, feeling alive and connected. And if you look at your life as a circle and all its aspects (family, finance, relationships, work, among others) as sections of it, you'll see that if one part is malfunctioning, it will affect the whole.

There have been many times in my life when I've put far too much emphasis on work and not nearly enough on taking care of me. There's a huge difference between attending to the needs of your personality (ego) and caring for your true self. Making that distinction can save you a lot of wasted time. This I know for sure.

You've got to be in touch with your mind, body, and spirit to live the life you were meant to. When all three are completely engaged, you're able to fulfill your potential on earth.

It's a decision you make: to pursue what you were called here to do and not just meander through your days. The average life expectancy for an American woman is 80. That's a prediction, not a promise. What you do today creates every tomorrow.

To own the abundant life that's waiting for you, you've got to be willing to do the real work. Not your job. Not your career profile. But heeding your spirit, which is whispering its greatest desires for you. You've got to get silent sometimes to hear it. And check in regularly. You must feed your mind with thoughts and ideas that open you to new possibilities. (When you stop learning, you cease to grow, and subconsciously tell the universe you've done it all—nothing new for you. So why are you here?)

You can't pretend that your body will function forever no matter how you treat it. Your body wants to move; it wants to be fed well. If you're sprinting through life as though it's a race you have to win, you need to slow down and schedule some rest. Because the truth is, you've already won. You're still here, with another chance to get it right, do better, and be better—starting now.

South Dublin Libraries

www.southdublinlibraries.ie

Y ears ago on my show, a young mother shared her frustration with getting her son to go to bed. Her son was 3 years old and ruling the house. He wanted to sleep in her bed; he refused even to lie down in his own. And the more the mother insisted, the more the child resisted—yelling and screaming, until he literally dropped from exhaustion.

We showed a tape of the two of them battling it out. When our expert, Dr. Stanley Turecki, finished watching, he said something that made the hairs on my arms stand up: "Nothing happens until you decide." The reason this 3-year-old boy didn't sleep in his own bed was that his mother had not decided it would happen. When she did, the child would go to his bed. He might cry and scream and rant until he fell asleep, but he would eventually realize that his mother had made up her mind.

Well, I knew Dr. Turecki was speaking about a 3-year-old, but I also knew for sure that this brilliant piece of advice applied to many other aspects of life. Relationships.

Career moves. Weight issues. Everything depends on your decisions.

When you don't know what to do, my best advice is to do nothing until clarity comes. Getting still, being able to hear your own voice and not the voices of the world, quickens clarity. Once you decide what you want, make a commitment to that decision.

One of my favorite quotes is from mountaineer W. H. Murray:

> Until one is committed there is hesitancy, the chance to draw back, always ineffectiveness. Concerning all acts of initiative (and creation), there is one elementary truth, the ignorance of which kills countless ideas and splendid plans: that the moment one definitely commits oneself, then Providence moves, too. All sorts of things occur to help one that would never otherwise have occurred. A whole stream of events issues from the decision, raising in one's favor all manner of unforeseen incidents and meetings and material assistance, which no man could have dreamt would have come his way. I have learned a

deep respect for one of Goethe's couplets: "Whatever you can do, or dream you can, begin it. / Boldness has genius, power, and magic in it."

Make a decision and watch your life move forward.

I'm *always fascinated by* lists of "Most Powerful People," and by the ways they use external things—fame, status, wealth—to define and rank power. It's curious how a person can go from the top of the list one year to unlisted the next—all in the blink of a board meeting. Was that person's power real, or was the power only in the position? We often get the two confused.

When I think of authentic power, I think of the power that occurs when purpose aligns with personality to serve the greater good. For me, the only real power is the kind that comes from the core of who you are and reflects all that you were meant to be. When you see this kind of power shining through someone in all its truth and certainty, it's irresistible, inspiring, elevating.

The secret is alignment: when you know for sure that you're on course and doing exactly what you're supposed to be doing, fulfilling your soul's intention, your heart's desire. When your life is on course with its purpose, you are at your most powerful. And though you may stumble, you will not fall.

I *went down to Louisiana* five days after Katrina hit to witness for myself the disastrous effects of the hurricane. Maya Angelou described it so profoundly, saying, "The land became water, and the water thought it was God."

I spent no more than ten minutes in the Superdome in New Orleans, where thousands of families had waited and waited for five days for help to come. Days afterward, I thought I could still smell the urine and feces, mixed with the pungency of decaying flesh.

I said on the air, "I think we all—this country—owe these families an apology."

The next day, Gayle King, who, in addition to being my best friend, is also O magazine's editor at large, got a phone call from an irate reader canceling her subscription because "Oprah has gotten too big for her britches, telling us the government needs to apologize to those people."

What I know for sure is that behind every catastrophe, there are great lessons to be learned. One of the greatest: As long as we play the "us and them" game, we don't evolve as people, as a nation, as a planet. Katrina gave us an opportunity to live in the space of an open heart and to show our compassion.

Over the years, I've heard many people lamenting why God allows this or that. Another lesson: People suffer not because of what God does but because of what we do and do not do.

So much of what happened in the aftermath of Katrina was man-made. And as we all saw, there was plenty of blame to go around. But the storm also gave us a chance to see that in moments of desperation, fear, and helplessness, each of us can be a rainbow of hope, doing what we can to extend ourselves in kindness and grace to one another. Because I know for sure that there is no *them*—there's only *us*.

I n January 2009 I appeared on the cover of O twice: two versions of me standing side by side, a before and after. In one image, the before, I was in good shape. In the after, I was overweight. I had the confidence to show these photos of myself because I knew I wasn't alone. An estimated 66 percent of American adults are either overweight or obese. And almost nobody's happy about it.

That cover stirred an outpouring of emotion and an avalanche of support. One of the most memorable responses I got was this e-mail from a friend: "Here's how I see your weight—it is your smoke detector. And we're all burning up the best part of our lives."

I'd never thought of it that way before, but it was a true aha moment. My weight was an indicator warning, a flashing light blaring my disconnection from the center of myself.

What I now know for sure is that for me weight is a spiritual issue, not a food issue. Marianne Williamson struck a nerve when she sent this e-mail: "Your weight is really an invitation to your best life."

All those years of diets doomed to fail, I thought weight was the barrier. I told myself I had a weight "problem"—instead of looking at my out-of-balance existence and how I used food to repress the facts.

I once coauthored a book with Bob Greene called *Make the Connection*. The title was his idea. Even while writing my part, which involved sharing my frustrated journal entries about being fat (I was 237 pounds when Bob and I met), I would often say to him, "Remind me again—what's the connection?"

I did learn from Bob that my overeating wasn't about potato chips, that I needed to peel back the layers of my addiction to food and figure out what was eating me. Obviously, I didn't peel deeply enough.

But now I know that the connection is loving, honoring, and protecting everything about yourself. Bob has often said to me, "Your weight is ultimately tied to your feelings of unworthiness." For years, I vehemently disagreed, saying, "Listen, Bob Greene, I'm not one of those people who think they don't deserve what they have. I've worked hard for everything I own."

But as I move along the spiritual path to permanently resolving and managing the weight issue, I now see that a sense of unworthiness can come in many forms.

I've been an overachiever since I was 3 years old. For years I felt the need to show that I belonged here—the need to prove my worth. I worked hard. I got A's. I won speaking contests, earned scholarships. I was in my mid-thirties before I realized that just being born makes you worthy enough to be here. I had nothing to prove.

For most of us who overeat, extra pounds correspond to unresolved anxieties, frustrations, and depressions, which all come down to fear we haven't worked through. We submerge the fear in food instead of feeling it and dealing with it. We repress it all with offerings from the fridge.

If you can conquer the fear, you'll fly. That's another "for sure."

Let your life awaken in you. Whatever your challenge—overeating, overindulging in any substance or activity, the loss of a relationship, money, position—let it be an open door to your holiest revelations about yourself, an invitation to your best life.

I *love to watch* the sun set over Maui, transforming the sky. Nature has an easier time with transformation than we earthly beings do.

Evolving as a human being is a lifelong excavation process—digging deep to uncover your underlying issues. Sometimes it feels like trying to shovel through Kilimanjaro. You keep hitting rock.

What I've discovered, though: Rocks unattended turn into mounds, and then mountains. And it's our job to do daily cleanups—in our work, our family, our relationships, our finances, our health.

Ignoring problems is easier, for sure, but if we take even tiny steps to address them, those steps eventually become giant leaps on the journey to self-actualization.

Reaching your potential as a person is more than an idea. It's the ultimate goal. The wonders we're capable of have nothing to do with the measurement of mankind, the lists of what's in and what's out, who's hot and who's not.

I'm talking about the real deal: Whose life did you touch? Who did you love, and who loved you back?

This I know for sure is what matters. For me, it's the only goal worth aiming for: a transformation of consciousness that allows me to know that I am no better or worse than any other being. That I simply am.

I n the third grade, I learned the Golden Rule: Do unto others as you would have them do unto you. I loved those words. I wrote them on everything and carried them around in my book satchel.

I was a good-deed doer. At one point, I even thought I was going to be a missionary. Every Sunday, I would go to church, sit second pew to the right, take out a notepad, and write down everything the minister said. At school the next day, I would recite the sermon on the playground. I called it Monday-morning devotion. The other 8-year-olds would see me coming and say, "Here comes that preacher." Back then, when the Progressive Missionary Baptist Church was trying to raise money for the poor children of Costa Rica, I started a campaign. I was going to collect more money than anyone else. I gave up my lunch money and convinced my classmates to do the same. It was all part of the principle of "Do unto others" that I lived by.

Then, in the fifth grade, I ran into some problems. There was a girl in my class who didn't like me, so I went around school talking about her. One of my friends pointed out that if I believed in doing unto others and was talking about this girl, chances are she was talking about me, too. "I don't care," I replied, "because I don't like her, anyway."

For a long time, whenever I would say or do something that went against my better self, I would try to justify it to myself. What I didn't understand is that all of our actions, both good and bad, come back to us. But eventually I learned that we receive from the world what we give to the world. I understand it from physics as the third law of motion: For every action, there's an equal and opposite reaction. It is the essence of what Eastern philosophers call karma. In *The Color Purple*, the character Celie explained it to Mister: "Everything you try to do to me, already done to you."

Your actions revolve around you as surely as the earth revolves around the sun.

This is why, when people say they're looking for happiness, I ask, "What are you giving to the world?" It's like the wife who once appeared on my show wondering why her relationship with her husband had broken down. She kept saying, "He used to make me so happy. He doesn't make me happy anymore." What she couldn't see was that she was the cause of her own effect. Happiness is never something you get from other people. The happiness you feel is in direct proportion to the love you are able to give.

If you think something is missing in your life or you're not getting what you deserve, remember that there's no Yellow Brick Road. You lead life; it doesn't lead you.

See what comes into your life when you spend extra time with your children. Let go of your anger with your boss or coworker and see what gets returned. Be loving to yourself and others and see that love reciprocated. This rule works every time, whether or not you are aware of it. It occurs in little things, big things, and the biggest things.

Today I try to do well and be well with everyone I encounter. I make sure to use my life for goodwill. Because I know for sure that what I think, what I say, what I do—everything will be returned to me. And the same is true for you.

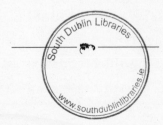